LOVE LANGUAGE MINUTE FOR COUPLES

LOVE LANGUAGE

— MINUTE —

for couples

100 DAYS TO A CLOSER RELATIONSHIP

GARY CHAPMAN

TYNDALE
MOMENTUM®

The nonfiction imprint of
Tyndale House Publishers, Inc.

Visit Tyndale online at www.tyndale.com.

Visit Tyndale Momentum online at www.tyndalemomentum.com.

TYNDALE, *Tyndale Momentum, The One Year*, and Tyndale's quill logo are registered trademarks of Tyndale House Publishers, Inc. The Tyndale Momentum logo, *One Year*, and the One Year logo are trademarks of Tyndale House Publishers, Inc. Tyndale Momentum is the nonfiction imprint of Tyndale House Publishers, Inc., Carol Stream, Illinois.

Love Language Minute for Couples: 100 Days to a Closer Relationship

Copyright © 2019 by Gary D. Chapman. All rights reserved.

Devotional content adapted from *The One Year Love Language Minute Devotional* published by Tyndale House Publishers under ISBN 978-1-4143-2973-4 in 2009.

Cover illustration of color smear copyright © vpanteon/Adobe Stock. All rights reserved.

Interior illustration of geometric patterns copyright © Youandigraphics/Creative Market. All rights reserved.

Author photograph copyright © by Boyce Shore & Associates. All rights reserved.

Unless otherwise indicated, all Scripture quotations are taken from the *Holy Bible*, New Living Translation, copyright © 1996, 2004, 2015 by Tyndale House Foundation. Used by permission of Tyndale House Publishers, Inc., Carol Stream, Illinois 60188. All rights reserved.

Scripture quotations marked ESV are from the ESV® Bible (The Holy Bible, English Standard Version®), copyright © 2001 by Crossway, a publishing ministry of Good News Publishers. Used by permission. All rights reserved.

Scripture quotations marked KJV are taken from the *Holy Bible*, King James Version.

Scripture quotations marked NIV are taken from the Holy Bible, *New International Version,*® *NIV.*® Copyright © 1973, 1978, 1984, 2011 by Biblica, Inc.® Used by permission. All rights reserved worldwide.

Scripture quotations marked NKJV are taken from the New King James Version,® copyright © 1982 by Thomas Nelson, Inc. Used by permission. All rights reserved.

For information about special discounts for bulk purchases, please contact Tyndale House Publishers at csresponse@tyndale.com, or call 1-800-323-9400.

ISBN 978-1-4964-4030-3

Printed in China

25   24   23   22   21   20   19
7   6   5   4   3   2   1

INTRODUCTION

I'VE BEEN PRIVILEGED TO counsel couples for more than forty years. In that time, I've seen my share of marital struggles. But I have also seen, time and time again, the power of God to transform relationships. When two people commit to each other—and especially when they commit to communicating love to each other through the five love languages—positive change occurs.

Because my background is in marriage counseling, I tend to use the language of marriage when I write. Some of the issues I address are marriage specific. However, if you're a dating or engaged couple, I hope you will read this book too. There is plenty of helpful information for you as well. The building blocks of marriage—such as good communication, respect, unconditional love, and forgiveness—are foundational to any romantic relationship. And learning to identify and speak your loved one's love language will benefit a couple at any stage.

You can use this devotional individually or read it together as a couple. Use the prayer for each day as a starting point for your own prayer—whether you pray silently together or aloud. In just a minute or two, you can discover encouraging biblical insights that will help you improve and build your relationship.

Whether your relationship is strong or struggling, stable or challenging, my prayer is that this devotional will encourage you and give you renewed joy in each other. May your relationship be strengthened as you focus on loving and growing together.

Three things will last forever—faith, hope,
and love—and the greatest of these is love.
Let love be your highest goal!

1 CORINTHIANS 13:13–14:1

◆

*Lord, thank you for creating each of us so differently. Keep
me from assuming that my partner thinks and feels the way
I do. Please give me the patience to find out how I can most
effectively communicate love to my spouse.*

COMMUNICATING LOVE

AFTER MORE THAN FORTY YEARS of counseling couples, I'm convinced there are five different ways we speak and understand emotional love—five love languages. Each of us has a primary love language; one of the five speaks to us more profoundly than the other four.

Seldom do a husband and wife have the same love language. We tend to speak our own language, and as a result, we completely miss each other. Oh, we're sincere. We're even expressing love, but we're not connecting emotionally.

Sound familiar? Love doesn't need to diminish over time. The end of the famous "love chapter" of the Bible, 1 Corinthians 13, says that love is of great value and will last forever. In fact, the apostle Paul says that love should be our highest goal. But if you're going to keep love alive, you need to learn a new language. That takes discipline and practice—but the reward is a lasting, deeply committed relationship.

◆ ◆ ◆

Roys NEEDS: CLEANLINESS, NOURISHMENT, PHYSICAL BEAUTY,
4Y5ICAL INTIMACY, QUALITY TIME, SPIRITUAL CONNECTION. (LOVE, HONOR, SERVATITE.

ALEXA NEEDS: QUIETNESS, BOUNDARIES, CREATIVITY,
MIND BLOWING SEX, STRATIGIC TIME THAT RESULTS
IN FRUIT

Dear friends, since God loved us that much, we surely ought to love each other. No one has ever seen God. But if we love each other, God lives in us, and his love is brought to full expression in us.

1 JOHN 4:11-12

Father, help me to be a student of my spouse. I want to know how best to show my love. Please give me wisdom as I try to determine my beloved's love language.

LEARNING THE LOVE LANGUAGES

My RESEARCH INDICATES THAT there are five basic languages of love:

- Words of affirmation—using positive words to affirm the one you love
- Gifts—giving thoughtful gifts to show you were thinking about someone
- Acts of service—doing something that you know the other person would like
- Quality time—giving your undivided attention
- Physical touch—holding hands, kissing, embracing, putting a hand on the shoulder, or any other affirming touch

Out of these five, each of us has a primary love language. One of these languages speaks more deeply to us than the others. Do you know your love language? Do you know your spouse's?

Many couples earnestly love each other but do not communicate their love in an effective way. If you don't speak your spouse's primary love language, he or she may not feel loved, even when you are showing love in other ways.

The Bible makes it clear that we need to love each other as God loves us. The apostle John wrote that God's love can find "full expression" in us. If that's true for the church in general, how much more true is it for a couple? Finding out how your loved one feels love is an important step to expressing love effectively.

◆ ◆ ◆

DAY 3

I am giving you a new commandment: Love each other. Just as I have loved you, you should love each other. Your love for one another will prove to the world that you are my disciples.

JOHN 13:34-35

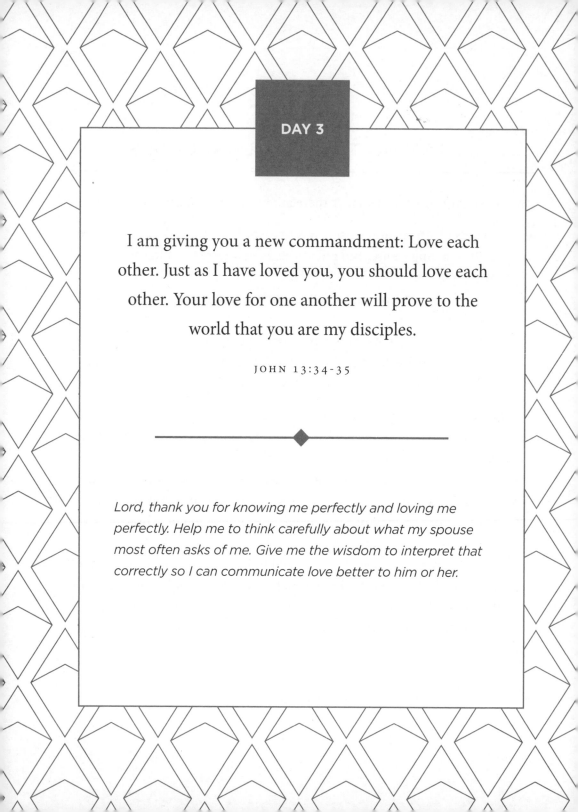

Lord, thank you for knowing me perfectly and loving me perfectly. Help me to think carefully about what my spouse most often asks of me. Give me the wisdom to interpret that correctly so I can communicate love better to him or her.

FOLLOWING THE CLUES

WHAT DOES YOUR SPOUSE most often request of you? This is usually a clue to a person's love language. You may have interpreted these requests as nagging, but in fact, your spouse has been telling you what makes him or her feel loved.

For example, if your mate frequently requests that you take a walk after dinner, go on a picnic, turn off the TV and talk, or go away for a weekend together, these are requests for *quality time*. One wife told me, "I feel neglected and unloved because my husband seldom spends time with me. He gives me nice gifts on my birthday and wonders why I'm not excited about them. Gifts mean little when you don't feel loved." Her husband was sincere and was trying to demonstrate his love, but he was not speaking her love language.

As we see from today's verse, Jesus instructed his disciples to love each other as he had loved them. How does God love us? Perfectly and with complete understanding. He knows us, and he knows how we can experience his love. We can never love perfectly this side of heaven, of course. But discovering the love language of your spouse is an important step in the right direction.

◆ ◆ ◆

The LORD gives righteousness and justice to all who are treated unfairly. He revealed his character to Moses and his deeds to the people of Israel.

PSALM 103:6-7

Father, help me to remember that revealing more of myself is the first step toward greater intimacy with the one I love. Thank you for revealing yourself to us, and please give me the courage to share myself with my spouse.

REVEALING YOURSELF IN MARRIAGE

WHAT DO YOU KNOW ABOUT the art of self-revelation? It all began with God. God revealed himself to us through the prophets, the Scriptures, and supremely through Christ. As today's verse mentions, he revealed himself to the ancient Israelites through his actions. They saw him guiding them out of Egypt and into the Promised Land, and as they did, they learned about him. If God had not chosen self-revelation, we would not know him.

The same principle is true in marriage. Self-revelation enables us to get to know each other's ideas, desires, frustrations, and joys. In a word, it is the road to intimacy. No self-revelation, no intimacy. So how do we learn the art of self-revelation?

You can begin by learning to speak for yourself. Communication experts often explain it as using "I" statements rather than "you" statements. For example, "*I* feel disappointed that you are not going with me to my mother's birthday dinner" is very different from "*You* have disappointed me again by not going to my mother's birthday dinner." When you focus on your reaction, you reveal your own emotions. Focusing on the other person's actions places blame. "You" statements encourage arguments. "I" statements encourage communication.

◆ ◆ ◆

For everything there is a season, a time for every activity under heaven. . . . A time to cry and a time to laugh. A time to grieve and a time to dance.

ECCLESIASTES 3:1, 4

Lord, expressing emotions does not always come easily to me. Help me to remember that holding back my feelings only makes my spouse guess why I'm acting the way I am. Please give me the courage to share what I am feeling. May it bring us closer together.

EXPRESSING FEELINGS

SOME PEOPLE WONDER WHY they would ever want to share their feelings with their mate. The truth is, if you don't openly share your feelings, they will likely show up anyway in your behavior. However, your loved one will have no idea why you are behaving as you are. That's when you get the proverbial question, "Is something wrong?" Your spouse knows something is wrong but doesn't know what.

Emotions are a natural part of life. King Solomon wrote in Ecclesiastes that there is a time for everything, including joy and sorrow, grieving and celebration. All feelings have their place in our lives, and many of them communicate a lot about us. Most of our feelings are tied to some experience we have had in the past or something we're going through now. The next time you feel disappointed, ask yourself, *What stimulated my disappointment?* Then try to share whatever it is with your spouse.

Revealing your feelings lets your spouse know what is going on inside you—what you are feeling and why. For example, you might say, "I'm feeling angry with myself because I came home late last night and we missed our ride in the country." Such a statement may encourage your mate to say, "I'm disappointed too. Maybe we can do it on Thursday night." Revealing your feelings creates an atmosphere of intimacy and trust.

❖ ❖ ❖

Hope deferred makes the heart sick, but
a dream fulfilled is a tree of life.

PROVERBS 13:12

◆

*Father, help me to communicate my desires more openly.
I don't want to be demanding, but I want to reveal more
of myself—and the things I hold close to my heart—to the
one I love. Please bless our relationship as we strive to fulfill
each other's desires.*

SHARING DESIRES

Now that we've looked at self-revelation, I want to talk about *sharing desires*. The failure to share desires is a source of much misunderstanding and frustration in any romantic relationship. Expecting your mate to fulfill your unexpressed desires is asking the impossible, and that makes disappointment inevitable. If you want your spouse to do something special on your birthday, for example, then say so. Don't expect your partner to read your mind.

In Proverbs 13:12, King Solomon presented a striking word picture of fulfilled and unfulfilled desires. Of course, not all our daily wishes rise to the level of making us heartsick if they're not fulfilled, but the basic idea is that when good, healthy desires are filled, joy can result. Why wouldn't you want to do that for your spouse? And why wouldn't your spouse want that for you?

Letting your spouse know what you want is a vital part of self-revelation. Several statements reveal desires: "I want . . . ," "I wish . . . ," "Do you know what would really make me happy?" or "I'd like to . . ." If you express your desires, your spouse has a chance to accommodate them. You are not demanding; you are requesting. You cannot control your spouse's decisions. You can clearly state what you would like. It's a step toward intimacy.

◆ ◆ ◆

O Lord, you have examined my heart and know everything about me. You know when I sit down or stand up. You know my thoughts even when I'm far away. . . . Such knowledge is too wonderful for me, too great for me to understand!

PSALM 139:1-2, 6

◆

Lord Jesus, thank you that you know us completely and love us anyway. Help us as a couple to aspire to a deeper knowledge of each other. Please encourage us as we learn to share about our behavior.

EXPLAINING OUR BEHAVIOR

TODAY'S VERSES FROM PSALM 139 are some of the best loved in Scripture because they reveal that God knows us inside and out. He knows our thoughts, our feelings, and why we do the things we do. We can't even comprehend that level of understanding, much less reproduce it. That's why self-revelation is so important for a couple.

We've talked about sharing desires and emotions, but it's important to share about our behavior as well. Your spouse can observe your behavior, but he or she may not interpret it correctly unless you explain it. For example, my wife may observe that I dozed off while she was talking to me. It would be helpful for me to say, "I nodded off on you. I'm sorry. I took a pill for my headache, and it is making me sleepy. It's not that I don't want to hear what you have to say." That explanation helps her understand my behavior correctly.

Explaining your behavior ahead of time can also be helpful. "I plan to mow the lawn as soon as I get home from the ball game. Okay? I love you." Now, she doesn't have to fret all afternoon about the long grass while you are off to the ball game. She knows what you intend to do.

Revealing past behavior can also give your spouse valuable information. "Today I went by the furniture store and looked at a bedroom set. I really like it, and I think it is a good deal. I'd like for you to look at it." Explaining what you've done regarding a decision or request helps your spouse process it appropriately. All these things promote understanding and intimacy for you as a couple.

Why worry about a speck in your friend's eye when you have a log in your own? . . . First get rid of the log in your own eye; then you will see well enough to deal with the speck in your friend's eye.

MATTHEW 7:3, 5

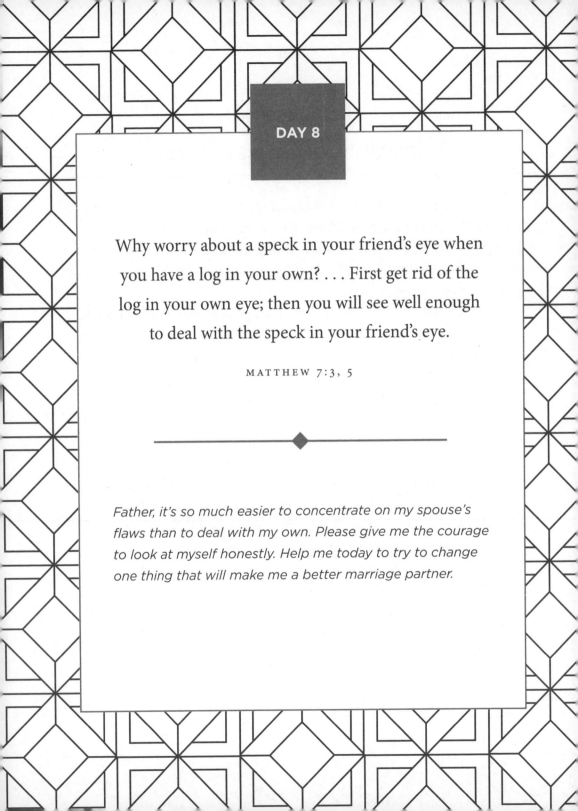

Father, it's so much easier to concentrate on my spouse's flaws than to deal with my own. Please give me the courage to look at myself honestly. Help me today to try to change one thing that will make me a better marriage partner.

WHERE CHANGE BEGINS

AS A MARRIAGE COUNSELOR, I've drawn one conclusion: Everyone wishes his or her spouse would change. "We could have a good marriage if he would just help me more around the house." Or "Our marriage would be great if she was willing to have sex more than once a month." He wants her to change, and she wants him to change. The result? Both feel condemned and resentful.

Jesus' words in Matthew 7 vividly illustrate the problem. We think we see others' faults clearly, and we put forth a lot of effort to try to correct them. But the truth is, our own sin blinds us. If we haven't dealt with our own failings, we have no business criticizing our spouse's.

There is a better way: *Start with yourself.* Admit that you're not perfect. Confess some of your most obvious failures to your spouse and acknowledge that you want to change. Ask for one suggestion each week on how you could be a better husband or wife. To the best of your ability, make changes. Chances are, your spouse will reciprocate.

◆ ◆ ◆

At last the wall was completed to half its height around the entire city, for the people had worked with enthusiasm.

NEHEMIAH 4:6

◆

Father God, thank you for the great example of teamwork from the book of Nehemiah. I want to keep our end goal in mind as my spouse and I negotiate the tasks in our home. Help me to do my part willingly and lovingly.

SHARING THE GOAL

As a couple, what is your shared goal? Perhaps it's a smoothly running home, a harmonious relationship, and a sense of fairness. Recently, a woman was in my office complaining that her husband didn't help her with household responsibilities. "We both work full-time," she said. "But he expects me to do everything around the house while he watches TV and unwinds. Well, maybe I need to unwind too." Clearly this couple had not defined their shared goal.

The players on an athletic team do not all perform the same tasks, but they do have the same goal. That was also true when Nehemiah led the Israelites to rebuild the wall around Jerusalem. Some of them rebuilt gates, some carried materials, and others stood guard, watching for those who wanted to sabotage the work. The individuals had separate tasks, but they were united in their ultimate goal: making the city of Jerusalem safe again.

If we want harmony and intimacy in our relationship, then we must each do our part of the work. A spouse who feels put upon is not likely to be interested in intimacy. Why not ask your spouse, "Do you feel that we make a good team around the house?" Let the answer guide your actions.

◆ ◆ ◆

[Jesus] looked around at them angrily and was deeply saddened by their hard hearts. Then he said to the man, "Hold out your hand." So the man held out his hand, and it was restored!

MARK 3:5

◆

Lord, thank you for emotions. You have made us in your image as emotional beings. Help me to look at my feelings as a gift. Please give me the wisdom to see the problem behind the emotion and deal with it before my strong feelings hurt my spouse.

EMBRACING EMOTIONS

SOME CHRISTIANS SEEM SUSPICIOUS and critical of emotions. Perhaps you've heard a statement like this one: "Don't trust your emotions. Faith, not feelings, is the road to spiritual growth." Why do we so disapprove of our emotions? In Mark 3 we read that Jesus felt anger and sorrow—and for good reason. It was the Sabbath, and when Jesus was in the synagogue, he noticed a man with a shriveled hand. He was compassionate and healed the man, but all the watching Pharisees could think about was that Jesus had broken their Sabbath laws. Jesus' anger and sorrow over their reaction was entirely appropriate and reflected the Father's own heart. Few of us would condemn Jesus for having those emotions. So why do we condemn ourselves?

God gave us emotions for growth, maturity, fulfillment, and enjoyment. Feelings were made to be our friends, and they can serve as important signals. When we experience a negative emotion, it tells us that something needs attention. Think of it like the dashboard light that appears when your car needs oil. We don't curse the light; we address the problem it's alerting us to. Why not do the same with your emotions? When you experience a negative emotion, especially regarding your spouse, stop for a moment and figure out the real problem. If you take constructive action, the emotion will have served its purpose.

◆ ◆ ◆

Sensible people control their temper;
they earn respect by overlooking wrongs.

PROVERBS 19:11

Lord, sometimes I experience so much anger over such little things. I know I'm hurting my spouse, and I don't want to do that anymore. Please forgive me. I release this anger to you. Help me to figure out why I have it and then let it go.

RELEASING ANGER

DO YOU FIND YOURSELF OVERREACTING to little irritations? Your spouse forgot the milk, and you grimace or make a sarcastic comment. Your child tracked mud on the new carpet, and you explode. If so, there is a good chance that you are suffering from stored anger—anger that has been living inside of you for years.

Perhaps your parents hurt you with harsh words or severe punishment. Maybe your peers made fun of you as a teenager or your boss treated you unfairly. If you've held all these hurts inside, now your stored anger may be showing up in your behavior. The Bible wisely tells us not to let the day end when we're still angry. In other words, we need to deal with our anger right away rather than letting it build up. In my book *Anger*, I talk about getting rid of stored anger. It all begins by releasing your anger to God. Tell him about your emotions and ask him to help you handle the situations that caused them. He can help you release the hurts from long ago and forgive those who wounded you.

Experiencing anger isn't wrong. But letting anger control us *is* wrong—and can be very damaging to a marriage.

◆ ◆ ◆

DAY 12

Always be humble and gentle. Be patient with each other, making allowance for each other's faults because of your love.

EPHESIANS 4:2

◆

Lord, I need more patience. Please teach me to let go of my expectations—for what others should be like, for what I should be able to accomplish, and for what I think I'm owed. Help me to treat my husband or wife with loving patience.

SHOWING PATIENCE

PATIENCE MEANS ACCEPTING THE imperfections of others. By nature, we want others to be as good as we are (or as good as we think we are), as on time as we are, or as organized as we are. The reality is, humans are not machines. The rest of the world does not live by our priority list; our agenda is not their agenda. It's especially important for couples to remember this. In a loving relationship, patience means bearing with our spouse's mistakes and giving him or her the freedom to be different from us.

When is the last time you were impatient with your significant other? Did your impatience come because he or she failed to live up to your expectations? I don't think it's coincidence that Ephesians 4:2 links humility with patience. When we're humble, we realize that the world doesn't revolve around us and that we don't set the standard for behavior. And when that's our mind-set, we're far less likely to become impatient.

The Bible says, "Love is patient and kind" (1 Corinthians 13:4). If in impatience you lash out at your loved one, love requires that you apologize and make it right. Work for more patience in your marriage.

◆ ◆ ◆

Fools think their own way is right,

but the wise listen to others.

PROVERBS 12:15

◆

Lord Jesus, thank you for listening to me when I pray. Help me to listen to my spouse—really listen—so I can understand him or her better.

LEARNING TO LISTEN

WE WILL NEVER RESOLVE CONFLICTS if we don't learn to listen. Many people think they are listening when in fact they are simply taking a break from talking—pausing to reload their verbal guns. Today's verse from Proverbs doesn't pull any punches when it calls those who don't listen *fools*. We may not like that word, but the truth is, refusing to listen reveals a lack of humility. Wise people listen to others—especially those they love. Genuine listening means seeking to understand what the other person is thinking and feeling. It involves putting ourselves in the other person's shoes and trying to look at the world through his or her eyes.

Here's a good sentence with which to begin: "I want to understand what you are saying because I know it is important." One man told me that he made a sign that read, "I am a listener." When his wife started talking, he would hang it around his neck to remind himself of what he was doing. His wife would smile and say, "I hope it's true." He learned to be a good listener.

◆ ◆ ◆

God showed how much he loved us by sending his one and only Son into the world so that we might have eternal life through him. This is real love—not that we loved God, but that he loved us and sent his Son as a sacrifice to take away our sins. Dear friends, since God loved us that much, we surely ought to love each other.

1 JOHN 4:9-11

Father, you have shown us the way to love—unconditionally, by taking the initiative and not waiting for the other person to reciprocate. Please help me to express that kind of love to my spouse.

TAKING THE INITIATIVE TO LOVE

I BELIEVE OUR DEEPEST EMOTIONAL NEED is the need to feel loved. If we are married, the person we most want to love us is our spouse. If we feel loved by our spouse, the whole world looks bright. If we do not feel loved, the whole world looks dark. However, we don't get love by complaining or making demands.

One man told me, "If my wife would just be a little more affectionate, then I could be responsive to her. But when she gives me no affection, I want to stay away from her." He is waiting to receive love before he gives love. Someone must take the initiative. Why must it be the other person?

Why are we so slow to understand that the initiative to love is always with us? God is our example. We love God because he first loved us (see 1 John 4:19). He loved us even when we were sinful, even when we weren't responsive, even when we had done nothing to deserve it. That's the ultimate example of love that takes the initiative. If you choose to give your spouse unconditional love and learn how to express love in a language your spouse can feel, there is every possibility that your spouse will reciprocate. Love begets love.

◆ ◆ ◆

A newly married man must not be drafted into the army or be given any other official responsibilities. He must be free to spend one year at home, bringing happiness to the wife he has married.

DEUTERONOMY 24:5

◆

Father, thank you for the gift of sex. As we seek to become closer sexually, help us to value each other's enjoyment as much as our own. Guide us in showing love to each other through sex.

MUTUAL SEXUAL FULFILLMENT

TWO QUESTIONS I HEAR FAIRLY OFTEN in my counseling practice are "How can I get my wife to have sex more often?" and "How can I make sure we both enjoy it?" How often a wife desires sex will be influenced by how her husband treats her. And finding mutual sexual fulfillment is a process; it doesn't happen automatically. In Deuteronomy 24:5, we read that God instructed the Israelites not to give a newly married man any official responsibilities, particularly those, such as military service, that would take him away from home. During the first year of marriage, couples were to bring happiness to each other. We can conclude that helping couples develop marital intimacy was important to God.

One of the best ways to learn about sexual intimacy is to seek out good information. I suggest that you and your spouse read one chapter each week in the book *The Gift of Sex* by Clifford and Joyce Penner. At the end of the week, discuss the ideas presented in the chapter. This is one way to better understand male and female sexuality and to discover how to give each other sexual pleasure.

Your attitude should always be one of love, looking out for each other's enjoyment. Share your desires with each other, but never force any particular sexual expression on your spouse. Open communication in an atmosphere of love will lead to mutual sexual fulfillment.

◆ ◆ ◆

Your love delights me, my treasure, my bride.
Your love is better than wine, your perfume more
fragrant than spices.

SONG OF SONGS 4:10

---

*Father, you know that sometimes I struggle with a
negative attitude toward sex. But I read in your Word
that sex is wholesome and good. Help me to believe that
wholeheartedly. Guide me as I talk with my spouse and try
to grow in this part of our marriage.*

POSITIVE VIEW OF SEX

I'D LIKE TO TALK ABOUT MAKING sex a mutual joy. Please note the word *mutual*. When it comes to sex, anything less than a deep sense of fulfillment on the part of both the husband and the wife is less than God intended. What, then, are the guidelines that lead us to such mutual satisfaction?

Number one is a healthy attitude toward sex. For any number of reasons, some people have very negative attitudes toward sexual intimacy, even within marriage. The answer to negative attitudes begins with a Bible study on sex. In 1 Corinthians 7, Paul affirms sex as an important part of marriage. If you read through the Song of Songs, you will see that married sex is celebrated in detail as a gift from God. Let this knowledge free you. After all, Jesus said, "If you remain faithful to my teachings . . . you will know the truth, and the truth will set you free" (John 8:31-32).

The second step toward changing your attitude is prayer. Ask God to transform your view of sex into a positive one. Positive attitudes lead to positive behavior.

◆ ◆ ◆

O my darling, lingering in the gardens,
your companions are fortunate to hear your voice.
Let me hear it, too!

SONG OF SONGS 8:13

◆

Lord God, you know that talking about sex is sometimes hard for me. Help me to remember that you want my relationship with my spouse to be strong in every area—including sex. Please give us grace to speak helpfully to each other as we talk about what we like and don't like in our sexual relationship.

COMMUNICATING ABOUT SEX

IF THERE IS ONE SKILL THAT IS MORE important than any other in gaining sexual oneness, it is *communication*. Why are we so ready to discuss everything else and so reticent to communicate openly about this area of marriage? When talking about sexuality, we should endeavor to follow the apostle Paul's advice and share helpful, encouraging words with each other. Your communication can make a dramatic difference to the level of mutual sexual satisfaction in your marriage.

Your wife will never know your feelings, needs, and desires if you do not express them. Your husband will never know what pleases you if you do not communicate. I have never known a couple who gained mutual sexual satisfaction without open communication about sexual matters. You cannot work on a problem of which you are unaware.

Let me share a practical idea to help you get started. At the top of a sheet of paper, write these words: "These are things I wish my spouse would do or not do to make the sexual part of our marriage better for me." Write down some ideas, and then share your lists with each other. Information opens the road to growth. Remember, your goal is making sex a mutual joy.

◆ ◆ ◆

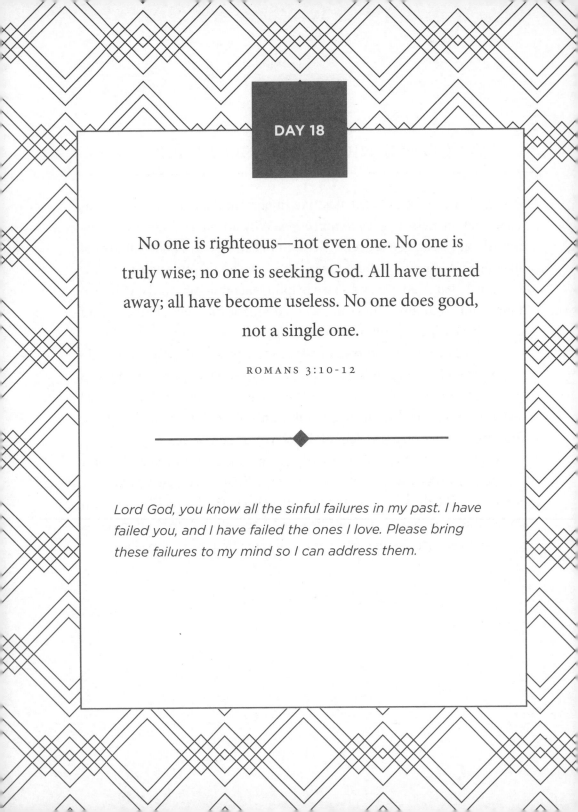

DAY 18

No one is righteous—not even one. No one is truly wise; no one is seeking God. All have turned away; all have become useless. No one does good, not a single one.

ROMANS 3:10-12

♦

Lord God, you know all the sinful failures in my past. I have failed you, and I have failed the ones I love. Please bring these failures to my mind so I can address them.

PAST FAILURES

DO YOU EVER WONDER WHY WE CAN'T just forget the past and move on? It's usually because we haven't dealt with the past appropriately. Harsh words and selfish attitudes may have left their mark on the soul of our relationship. But healing is available, and it begins with identifying past failures so we can confess them and ask forgiveness. The wall that has been built between you and your spouse must be torn down one block at a time. The first step is to identify the blocks.

Why not ask God to bring to your mind the times you have failed your spouse? Get your pencil ready and write them down. Then ask your spouse to make a list of the ways he or she thinks you have failed in the past. Consider asking your children or your parents to share times they have observed you speaking harshly or being unkind to your spouse. As you make your list, you may discover that the wall of past failures is high and thick. That's okay. The Bible is clear that everyone has sinned—against God and against others. Admitting and identifying past failure is the first step in "wall demolition."

◆ ◆ ◆

Make allowance for each other's faults, and forgive anyone who offends you. Remember, the Lord forgave you, so you must forgive others.

COLOSSIANS 3:13

Father, I am so grateful for your forgiveness. Help me to extend that same gracious forgiveness to my spouse when he or she requests it, even when that's hard. I know the benefits will be great.

FORGIVING EACH OTHER

When your spouse confesses past failures and requests your forgiveness, it is time to forgive. In fact, refusing to forgive violates the clear teaching of Jesus. He taught his disciples to pray to our heavenly Father: "Forgive us our sins, as we have forgiven those who sin against us" (Matthew 6:12). If we refuse to forgive when others confess to us and repent, we jeopardize our own forgiveness from God. The apostle Paul underscores this point in Colossians 3:13, where he writes that we must forgive others because the Lord has forgiven us. And one of Jesus' parables makes clear that our "forgiveness debt" to the Lord is far greater than the debt anyone can "owe" us (see Matthew 18:21-35).

Nothing is to be gained by holding on to past failures. By contrast, a willingness to forgive opens the door to the possibility of future growth. Trust can be rebuilt and love restored. When a couple is willing to confess and forgive past failures, a marriage can move from a place of bitterness and hardship to a place of renewal and joy.

◆ ◆ ◆

My heart has heard you say, "Come and talk with me." And my heart responds, "LORD, I am coming."

PSALM 27:8

◆

Father, thank you for wanting to talk to me and hear from me! I know that conversation builds relationships. Help me to share my thoughts freely with my loved one and listen carefully to his or her thoughts as well.

INTELLECTUAL INTIMACY

MOST OF US GOT MARRIED NOT BECAUSE we wanted someone to help us cook meals, wash dishes, maintain the car, and rear children. Rather, we married out of a deep desire to know and to be known, to love and to be loved, and to have a genuinely intimate relationship. How does this lofty goal become reality? It helps to look at the five essential components of an intimate relationship, which we'll do in the next several devotions.

First is intellectual intimacy. So much of life is lived in the world of the mind. Throughout the day, we have hundreds of thoughts about life as we encounter it. We also have desires, things we would like to experience or obtain. Intellectual intimacy comes from sharing some of these thoughts and desires with our spouse. These may focus on finances, food, health, current events, music, or church. Whether or not they're important in and of themselves, these thoughts and desires reveal something about what has gone on in our mind throughout the day.

Psalm 27:8 describes a way to increase our intimacy with God—by responding when he invites us to talk with him. The same principle applies to human relationships. In marriage, we have the pleasure of learning some of the inner movements of our spouse's mind. That is the essence of intellectual intimacy.

◆ ◆ ◆

I am bent over and racked with pain.
All day long I walk around filled with grief.

PSALM 38:6

◆

Lord, thank you for wanting to hear our feelings. I know sharing emotions as a couple will help us grow closer. I pray that you will help us cultivate a loving, accepting atmosphere where we can share freely.

EMOTIONAL INTIMACY

EMOTIONAL INTIMACY IS ONE of the five components of an intimate relationship. Feelings are our spontaneous, emotional responses to what we encounter through the five senses. I hear that the neighbor's dog died, and I feel sad. I see the fire truck racing down the road, and I feel troubled. My wife touches my hand, and I feel loved. I see her smile, and I feel encouraged.

Your inner life is filled with emotions, but no one sees them. Sharing your feelings builds emotional intimacy. Allowing your mate into your inner world means being willing to say, "I'm feeling a lot of fear right now" or "I am really happy tonight." These are statements of self-revelation. Psalm 38:6 gives just one of many examples of the psalmist pouring out his heart to God. King David and the other writers of the psalms were honest about their feelings of sadness, depression, anger, and grief, as well as their feelings of joy, adoration, and celebration. And that kind of straightforward self-revelation only increased their intimacy with God.

Learning to talk about emotions can be one of the most rewarding experiences in life. Such sharing requires an atmosphere of acceptance. If I am assured that my spouse will not condemn my feelings or try to change my feelings, then I am far more likely to talk about them.

◆ ◆ ◆

In the night I search for you [Lord];
in the morning I earnestly seek you.

ISAIAH 26:9

Lord Jesus, I am grateful for the memories we have developed as a couple. Thank you for fun and laughter and times we can just enjoy being together and doing things together. Help us to cultivate social intimacy as we grow in our relationship.

SOCIAL INTIMACY

MUCH OF LIFE CENTERS ON ENCOUNTERS that happen throughout the day—things people say or do or situations that develop. When my wife and I share these with each other, we feel that we are a part of what the other is doing. We develop social intimacy and sense that we are a social unit. In other words, what happens in my wife's life is important to me.

Another aspect of social intimacy involves the two of us doing things together. Attending a movie or athletic event, shopping or washing the car together, or having a picnic in the park are all ways of building social intimacy. Much of life involves doing. When we do things together, we are not only developing a sense of teamwork, but we are also enhancing our relationship. In the verse above, we see that the prophet Isaiah wrote about strongly desiring to spend time with God. That same sense of urgency to be in another's company—which often is prompted by our good memories of previous encounters—is beneficial in marriage.

The things we do together often form our most vivid memories. Will we ever forget climbing Mount Mitchell together? Or giving the dog a haircut? Social intimacy is an important part of a growing marriage.

◆ ◆ ◆

We also pray that you will be strengthened with all his glorious power so you will have all the endurance and patience you need. May you be filled with joy, always thanking the Father.

COLOSSIANS 1:11-12

Father, I know there is nothing more important in our lives than our relationship with you. Help me to be an encouragement to my spouse in this area. Let us be willing to share our thoughts and prayers with each other. Draw us closer to each other, Lord, as we draw closer to you.

SPIRITUAL INTIMACY

MARITAL INTIMACY HAS five essential components. We've talked about intellectual, emotional, and social intimacy, and today we'll look at spiritual intimacy. We are spiritual creatures. Anthropologists have discovered that people from cultures around the world are religious. We all have a spiritual dimension. The question is, are we willing to share this part of our lives with those we love? When we do, we experience spiritual intimacy.

It may be as simple as sharing something you read in the Bible this morning and what it meant to you. Spiritual intimacy is also fostered by shared experience. After attending a worship service with her husband, one wife said, "There is something about hearing him sing that gives me a sense of closeness to him." Praying together is another way of building spiritual intimacy. If you feel too awkward praying aloud, then pray silently while holding hands. No words are uttered, but your hearts move closer to each other.

You might also consider praying for each other as a way to strengthen your relationship. Many of Paul's epistles contain beautiful prayers for those to whom he was writing, including the one above from Colossians 1, which asks the Lord to strengthen the believers and give them patience, endurance, and joy. Praying passionately for your spouse's relationship with God can be a supremely intimate experience.

◆ ◆ ◆

The husband should fulfill his wife's sexual needs,
and the wife should fulfill her husband's needs.
The wife gives authority over her body to her
husband, and the husband gives authority
over his body to his wife.

1 CORINTHIANS 7:3-4

◆

*Father God, forgive me for the times when I've seen physical
satisfaction as the only goal of sex. Help us as a couple to
focus on the intimate, emotional connection that comes
when we think of each other in our sexual relationship.*

SEXUAL INTIMACY

BECAUSE MEN AND WOMEN ARE different sexually, we often pursue sexual intimacy in different ways. The husband's emphasis is most often on the physical aspects. Seeing, touching, feeling, and the experience of foreplay and climax are the focus of his attention. The wife, on the other hand, comes to sexual intimacy with an emphasis on the emotional aspect. To feel loved, cared for, appreciated, and treated tenderly brings her great pleasure. In short, if she truly feels loved, then the sexual experience is but an extension of this emotional pleasure.

Sexual intimacy requires an understanding response to these differences. In 1 Corinthians 7, the apostle Paul writes directly that each spouse should fulfill the other's sexual needs. In other words, sexual intimacy requires selflessness. For the sexual relationship to be a source of relational closeness, each spouse must think first of the other and how best to make sex a source of joy for him or her.

It should be obvious that we cannot separate sexual intimacy from emotional, intellectual, social, and spiritual intimacy. We cannot attain sexual intimacy without intimacy in the other areas of life. The goal is not just to have sex, but to experience closeness and to find a sense of mutual satisfaction.

◆ ◆ ◆

Understand this, my dear brothers and sisters:
You must all be quick to listen, slow to speak,
and slow to get angry.

JAMES 1:19

Lord Jesus, please help me to uncover why I get so defensive about certain things. And give me the wisdom to change my reaction. I know I also need to extend special patience and grace to my spouse when he or she becomes defensive. Help us to avoid each other's hot spots rather than triggering them.

DEALING WITH EMOTIONAL HOT SPOTS

WE ALL HAVE EMOTIONAL HOT SPOTS. When our spouse says or does certain things, we get defensive. Usually our response is rooted in our history. You may find that often your spouse is echoing statements made by your parents that hurt or embarrassed you. The fact that you get defensive indicates that the hurt has never healed. The next time you get defensive, ask yourself why. Chances are, you will have a flood of memories. Share these past experiences with your spouse, and he or she will develop greater understanding.

What if you are the spouse? Once you learn why your husband or wife gets defensive in a certain area, then you can decide how to move on. You might ask, "How would you like me to talk about this issue in the future? I don't want to hurt you. How could I say it in a way that would not be hurtful to you?" Now you are on the road to defusing the defensive behavior of your spouse. You're also following Scripture by being patient and making allowances for your spouse's struggles. Learning to negotiate the "hot spots" of life is a big part of developing a growing marriage.

◆ ◆ ◆

DAY 26

For everything there is a season . . .
a time to embrace and a time to turn away.

ECCLESIASTES 3:1, 5

Father God, thank you for the gift of physical touch. Help me to communicate my love to my spouse by the way I touch him or her.

PHYSICAL TOUCH

KEEPING EMOTIONAL LOVE ALIVE in a relationship makes life much more enjoyable. The husband or wife who feels loved is less likely to stray. How do we keep love alive after the "in love" emotions have evaporated? I believe it is by learning to speak each other's love language. Today, I want to focus on the love language of physical touch.

When some husbands hear the words *physical touch*, they immediately think of sex. But sexual intercourse is only one of the dialects of the love language physical touch. Holding hands, kissing, embracing, giving back rubs, putting an arm around the shoulder, or gently putting your hand on your loved one's leg are all ways of expressing love by physical touch. Solomon's Old Testament book Song of Songs makes it clear that physical touch between a husband and wife can be beautiful, intimacy building, and celebrated. Today's verse is just one example of the book's poetry celebrating physical expressions of love.

For some people, both men and women, physical touch is their primary love language. If you don't give them tender touch, they may not feel loved even though you are speaking other love languages. If this describes your spouse, make sure you work on meaningful touch.

◆ ◆ ◆

His left arm is under my head, and
his right arm embraces me.

SONG OF SONGS 2:6

◆

*Lord Jesus, please help me to learn how my spouse
wants to be touched. My love is so strong, and I want to
communicate that.*

LEARNING THE LANGUAGE OF TOUCH

To the person whose primary love language is physical touch, nothing is more important than tender touches. To touch my body is to touch me. To withdraw from my body is to distance yourself from me emotionally. In our society, shaking hands is a way of communicating openness and social politeness. When on rare occasions one person refuses to shake hands with another, it communicates that things are not right in their relationship. The same principle applies in marriage. Withdraw from your spouse physically, and you are withdrawing emotionally.

Touches may be explicit and call for your full attention, such as a back rub or sexual foreplay. Or they may be implicit and require only a moment, such as putting your hand on her shoulder as you pour a cup of coffee or rubbing your body against him as you pass in the kitchen. Once you discover that physical touch is the primary love language of your husband or wife, you are limited only by your imagination. Kiss when you get in the car. It may greatly enhance your travels. Give him a hug before you go shopping, and you may hear less griping when you return. Try new touches in new places and listen for feedback on whether it is pleasurable. Remember, your spouse has the final word; you are learning to speak his or her language.

◆ ◆ ◆

The one thing I ask of the LORD—the thing I seek most—is to live in the house of the LORD all the days of my life, delighting in the LORD's perfections and meditating in his Temple.

PSALM 27:4

Father, I know that your Kingdom should be my first priority, but too often that's not reflected in the way I live. Please forgive me. Help me to seek your Kingdom above all. May I have your perspective on every aspect of my life, including the way I think about marriage.

SEEKING HIS KINGDOM

A PRIORITY IS SOMETHING we believe to be important. When we list priorities, we are listing those things we believe to be of great value in life.

Most Christians would agree that priority number one is our relationship and fellowship with God. Nothing is more important. In fact, our relationship with God influences the rest of our priorities. If God is the author of life, then nothing is more important than knowing him. If God has spoken, then nothing is more important than hearing his voice. If God loves, nothing can bring greater joy than responding to his love. In Psalm 27:4, the psalmist voiced his highest desire: to seek God's face and be in his presence. Jesus said, "Seek first the kingdom of God and His righteousness" (Matthew 6:33, NKJV).

Can you honestly say that seeking the Kingdom of God is your first priority? If so, that will have a profound impact on the way you approach your marriage. To follow God's guidelines for marriage, as in all of life, will be your burning desire.

◆ ◆ ◆

"At last!" the man exclaimed. "This one is bone from my bone, and flesh from my flesh! She will be called 'woman,' because she was taken from 'man.'" This explains why a man leaves his father and mother and is joined to his wife, and the two are united into one.

GENESIS 2:23-24

Father, thank you for putting such a high priority on families. Help me to keep that priority in my own life and to realize how my actions toward my spouse will affect my children for years to come.

PRIORITIZING FAMILY

IS YOUR FAMILY ONE OF YOUR TOP PRIORITIES? When we recognize that God established marriage and family as the most basic unit of society, family becomes extremely important. In fact, Psalm 68:6 tells us that in his compassion, "God places the lonely in families."

Within family relationships, we recognize that the marriage relationship is more fundamental than the parent-child relationship. Today's verses from Genesis 2 show just how unique the husband-wife relationship is. Not only was the first woman created from the man's rib, but no other human relationship is described with such terms as "cleaving" or "becoming one." Marriage is a lifelong, intimate relationship. By contrast, most children will eventually leave their parents and establish their own families.

If family is one of my top priorities, how will that affect the way I spend my time, money, and energy? When I serve my wife, I am also doing something for my children. I'm setting an example that I hope they will remember when they get married. One of the most important things you can do for your children is to love and serve your spouse. Nothing creates a more secure environment for children than seeing Mom and Dad loving each other. And nothing else cements your marriage relationship quite so well.

◆ ◆ ◆

"A man leaves his father and mother and is joined to his wife, and the two are united into one." Since they are no longer two but one, let no one split apart what God has joined together.

MATTHEW 19:5-6

Lord, sometimes I get frustrated when I feel my spouse's family is more important to him or her than I am. Help me to avoid pointless arguing and instead focus on showing love. May we truly cleave to each other and be united in love.

WHEN FAMILY GETS IN THE WAY

A WOMAN ONCE ASKED ME, "We are supposed to leave our families and cleave to each other, but my husband is so attached to his family that I feel left out. What can I do?" Of course, this situation can happen with either women or men.

The concept of "leaving and cleaving" is central to the Bible's teaching on marriage. It first appears in Genesis, right after the very first woman and man were united. Both Jesus and Paul quoted this verse as well, and for good reason. When the principle isn't followed, marriages suffer.

If you find yourself in the circumstances of the woman I mentioned above, you will feel left out because your spouse is not meeting your emotional need for love. You might even feel that his family is more important to him than you are. However, the answer is not to blast your spouse with angry lectures about being overly attached to his parents. When you do that, you drive him away. His parents are giving him love while you are angry and demanding. You will argue endlessly about the time he spends with his parents—which is the symptom rather than the root problem. Your relationship will suffer.

A better approach is to focus on meeting each other's need for love. Leave the in-laws out of the discussion. Find out what makes your spouse feel loved, and share what makes you feel loved. Then concentrate on speaking the right love language. You and your spouse will be drawn together as you begin to feel loved by each other. Spending time with each other will become even more appealing than spending time with your parents, and your relationship will be strengthened.

The heart of the discerning acquires knowledge,
for the ears of the wise seek it out.

PROVERBS 18:15 (NIV)

◆

Lord Jesus, I want to be an empathetic listener rather than a judgmental one. Please help me to concentrate on my spouse when we're talking rather than on myself. Bless our conversations.

LISTENING WITH EMPATHY

THE ABILITY TO *SPEAK* AND TO *LISTEN* are two of the more profound gifts of God. Nothing is more fundamental to a relationship than talking and listening. Open communication is the lifeblood that keeps a marriage in the spring and summer seasons—times of optimism and enjoyment. Conversely, failure to communicate is what brings on fall and winter—times of discouragement and negativity.

It sounds so simple. The problem is that many of us tend to be judgmental listeners. We evaluate what we hear based on our own view of the situation, and we respond by pronouncing our judgment. And then we wonder why our spouse doesn't talk more.

For most of us, effective listening requires a significant change of attitude. We must shift from *egocentric* listening (viewing the conversation through our own eyes) to *empathetic* listening (viewing the conversation through our partner's eyes). The goal is to discover how our spouse perceives the situation and how he or she feels. Proverbs 18:15 equates wisdom with careful listening and seeking for knowledge. In a relationship, this often means seeking knowledge about our spouse. Words are a key to the other person's heart. Listening with the intention to understand enhances conversation.

◆ ◆ ◆

Clothe yourselves with tenderhearted mercy,
kindness, humility, gentleness, and patience.

COLOSSIANS 3:12

*Father, let me make it my goal to give a gentle answer to
my spouse. Please give me the humility to acknowledge his
or her feelings without immediately needing to point out
my perspective.*

AFFIRMING IN DISAGREEMENT

DO YOU KNOW HOW TO AFFIRM your spouse even when you disagree? It's a big step in learning how to have meaningful conversations. Take this example: A wife has shared that she is hurt by something her husband has done, and he responds, "I appreciate your sharing your ideas and feelings with me. Now I can understand why you could feel so hurt. If I were in your shoes, I'm sure I would feel the same way. I want you to know that I love you very much, and it hurts me to see you upset. I appreciate your being open with me." This husband has learned the art of affirming his wife even though he may not agree with her perception.

Of course, he has a perspective and will eventually share it, but first, he wants his wife to know that he understands what she is saying and can identify with her pain. He is not condemning her interpretation, nor is he telling her that she should not feel upset. In fact, he is acknowledging that if he were in her shoes, he would feel the same way. And he would— because if he had her personality and perception, then he would feel what she feels.

Harsh words or judgment will frequently provoke anger. But giving a gentle answer, as King Solomon says in today's proverb, encourages a thoughtful response. This affirmation of feelings creates a positive climate where the offended person can now hear the other person's side.

◆ ◆ ◆

This is my commandment: Love each other in the same way I have loved you. There is no greater love than to lay down one's life for one's friends.

JOHN 15:12-13

◆

Lord Jesus, thank you for demonstrating for us the greatest kind of love. I'm in awe of your willingness to lay down your life for me. Thank you. Please help me to respond with a humble willingness to lay down my life for my spouse, even in smaller ways such as communicating in his or her love language.

WHEN IT DOESN'T COME NATURALLY

I'M OFTEN ASKED, "What if your spouse's love language is something that doesn't come naturally for you?" Maybe his love language is *physical touch*, and you're just not a toucher. Or *gifts*, but gifts are not important to you. Perhaps her love language is *quality time*, but sitting on the couch and talking for twenty minutes is your worst nightmare. He wants *words of affirmation*, but words don't come easily for you. Or she prefers *acts of service*, but you don't find satisfaction in keeping the house organized. So, what are you to do?

You learn to speak your partner's language. If it doesn't come naturally for you, learning to speak it is an even greater expression of love because it shows effort and a willingness to learn. This speaks volumes to your spouse. Also, keep in mind that your love language may not come naturally for your loved one. Your spouse has to work just as hard to speak your language as you do to speak his or her language. That's what love is all about.

Jesus made it clear that we are to love each other as he loved us—and that is with the highest degree of sacrifice. Few of us are called to literally lay down our lives for others, but we are called to lay down our lives in small ways every day. Love is giving. Choosing to speak love in a language that is meaningful to your spouse is a great investment of your time and energy.

◆ ◆ ◆

Both day and night belong to you [Lord]; you made the starlight and the sun. You set the boundaries of the earth, and you made both summer and winter.

PSALM 74:16-17

Lord, you have created different seasons of the earth, and we can see different seasons of our lives. But I know you did not create us to be in cold, wintry relationships. Encourage us as a couple to renew the hope and optimism we have for our relationship.

SEASONS OF MARRIAGE

THE BIBLE TELLS US THAT GOD has created all the boundaries of the earth, including the rotation around the sun, which causes seasonal changes. The seasons come and go: winter, spring, summer, and fall. So do the seasons of marriage. Relationships are perpetually in a state of transition, continually moving from one season to another. But the seasons of marriage don't always follow the order of nature. You may be in a spring marriage today and in a winter marriage next month. What do the seasons of marriage look like?

Sometimes we find ourselves in winter—discouraged, detached, and dissatisfied. Other times we experience springtime with its openness, hope, and anticipation. On still other occasions, we bask in the warmth of summer—comfortable, relaxed, enjoying life. And then comes fall with its uncertainty, negligence, and apprehension. The cycle repeats itself many times throughout the life of a marriage, just as the seasons repeat themselves in nature.

In the next few days, we will look at these recurring seasons of marriage and help you identify which season your marriage is in. I will also suggest ways to enhance the seasons of marriage. You're never "stuck" in one season; you can make positive changes.

◆ ◆ ◆

The heartfelt counsel of a friend is as
sweet as perfume and incense.

PROVERBS 27:9

◆

*Father, when our relationship is in trouble, filled with
rejection and discouragement, help us to find a wise
adviser. Give us the grace and energy to work on
rejuvenating the love between us.*

FIGHTING WINTER

TELL ME YOUR EMOTIONS, YOUR ATTITUDES, and your behavior toward your spouse, and I'll tell you the season of your marriage. Today we focus on the winter marriage.

What are the emotions of winter? Hurt, anger, disappointment, loneliness, and rejection. What are the attitudes of a winter marriage? In a word, negativity. You might hear things such as "I'm so discouraged with my marriage." "It's such a frustration." "I don't know if we're going to be able to work things out."

What are the actions in a winter marriage? Speaking harshly or not speaking at all, destructive and perhaps violent behavior. In the winter season of marriage, couples are unwilling to negotiate differences. Conversations turn to arguments. There is no sense of togetherness. The marriage is like two people living in separate igloos.

The good news is that a winter marriage often makes couples desperate enough to break out of their suffering and seek the help of a counselor or pastor. The book of Proverbs refers to heartfelt counsel from someone who cares for us as very sweet. Good advice is highly valuable, and often the perspective of someone outside the relationship is critical for people who really want to change. Those who seek help will find it.

◆ ◆ ◆

Remember this—a farmer who plants only a few seeds will get a small crop. But the one who plants generously will get a generous crop.

2 CORINTHIANS 9:6

Father, I remember times of spring in my marriage, and I want that again. Please rekindle in us a sense of excitement and optimism. Help us to put in the time and effort to plant seeds in our relationship—that we may reap a good return.

SEEDS FOR SPRING

A SPRING MARRIAGE IS FILLED WITH HOPE, anticipation, optimism, gratitude, love, and trust. Does that sound exciting? It is! Some of you are saying, "I remember the early days of our marriage when we were in spring." I want to suggest that you can have spring again and again. A healthy marriage will have many spring seasons throughout the years.

How do couples create this kind of climate? By making plans and communicating openly. Those who want to live in a spring relationship are willing to seek the help of a counselor or read a relevant book. Spring is a time of new beginnings, when the streams of communication are flowing. A couple feels a sense of excitement about life together. They have great hopes for the future, and they are planting seeds from which they hope to reap a harvest of happiness. The above verse from 2 Corinthians gives us this promise: If we plant generously, we will experience a good return on our work. Those who plant seeds will see the flowers of spring.

◆ ◆ ◆

Live in harmony with each other. . . . Do things in such a way that everyone can see you are honorable. Do all that you can to live in peace with everyone.

ROMANS 12:16-18

♦

Father, thank you for a comfortable, positive relationship with my spouse. Even though I am grateful for the peace between us, let me not seek that at the expense of genuine resolution of our problems. Help me to deal with them lovingly.

RELAXATION OF SUMMER

IN A SUMMER MARRIAGE, there are feelings of happiness, satisfaction, accomplishment, and connection. There is a deep level of trust and a commitment to growth. Life is more relaxed, and communication is constructive. A couple in this stage is likely attending marriage conferences periodically, reading books, and growing spiritually.

The climate of a summer marriage is comfortable, supportive, and understanding. The couple resolves conflicts in a positive manner. Having accepted their differences, they seek to turn them into assets, utilizing their differences to help each other. In summer, husbands and wives have a growing sense of togetherness.

If there is one downside to summer, it is *yellow jackets*. They live underground and represent those unresolved issues that have been pushed beneath the surface to preserve the peace. Remember the Bible's wise instruction to deal with anger right away. Letting things fester, even in the name of peacemaking, only makes things worse. Ultimately, you must deal with the yellow jackets or your summer marriage will be headed toward fall.

◆ ◆ ◆

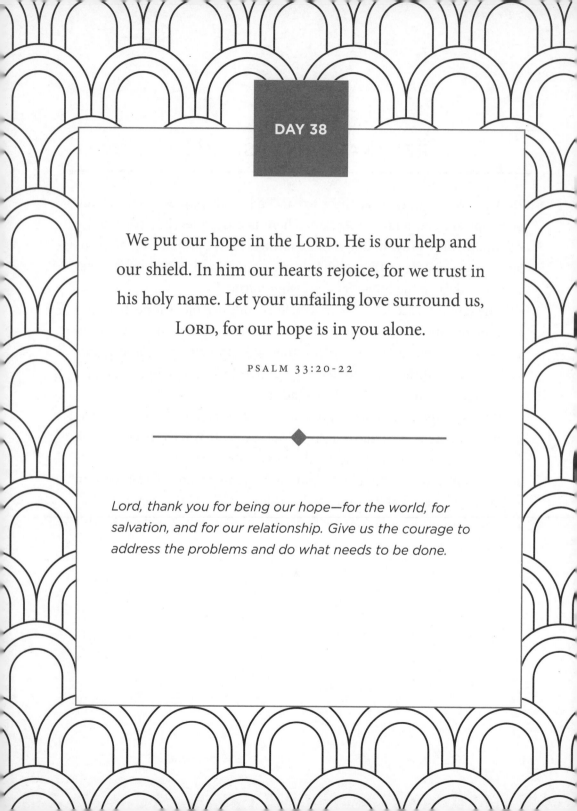

DAY 38

We put our hope in the LORD. He is our help and our shield. In him our hearts rejoice, for we trust in his holy name. Let your unfailing love surround us, LORD, for our hope is in you alone.

PSALM 33:20-22

◆

Lord, thank you for being our hope—for the world, for salvation, and for our relationship. Give us the courage to address the problems and do what needs to be done.

WAKE-UP CALL OF FALL

IN THE FALL WHERE I LIVE IN NORTH CAROLINA, the leaves begin to change colors and eventually fall off the trees. That is what happens in a fall marriage. It may look good on the outside, but actually it is falling apart. In the fall season, couples sense that something is happening, but they're not sure what. One or both spouses begin to feel neglected. They are disengaging emotionally.

In a fall marriage, you begin to feel sadness, apprehension, discouragement, fear, and eventually resentment. You have neglected your relationship and have drifted apart. There is a growing concern, uncertainty, and a tendency to blame each other.

The fall season of marriage is a wake-up call to seek help: See a counselor or pastor, read a book, or attend a class. Unlike the real seasons, marriages can move from fall to spring without going through winter; but you must take action to make that happen. If you don't, you will soon be in the coldness of winter.

The Bible reassures us that there is always hope. Trust in the Lord as your help, and let his love surround you and encourage you that better days can be ahead.

◆ ◆ ◆

Respect everyone, and love the family of believers.

1 PETER 2:17

◆

Father, please forgive me for the times I have been disrespectful to my spouse in the way I talk. I have not listened; I have been demanding and controlling, and have breached confidences. I know that kind of behavior is not loving. I pray that you would help me commit to a new, better way of communicating.

RESPECTFUL COMMUNICATION

I'VE HEARD MANY PEOPLE SAY, "My spouse won't talk with me." If this describes your marriage, the question is, why? One reason some spouses go silent is negative communication patterns. Here are some question to help you think about your own patterns. Consider whether you often come across as negative or complaining.

- Do I listen to my spouse when he talks, or do I cut him off and give my responses?
- Do I allow my partner space when she needs it, or do I force the issue of communication, even at those times when she needs to be alone?
- Do I maintain confidences, or do I broadcast our private conversations to others?
- Do I openly share my own needs and desires in the form of requests rather than demands?
- Do I give my spouse the freedom to have opinions that differ from my own, or am I quick to "set him straight"?

If you answer yes to the second half of any of these questions, it may be time to change your communication patterns. It's all about treating your spouse (and all believers) with respect and love, as 1 Peter 2:17 directs. Doing so may loosen the tongue of a silent spouse.

◆ ◆ ◆

Let everything you say be good and helpful, so that
your words will be an encouragement to
those who hear them.

EPHESIANS 4:29

◆

*Lord God, as I seek to grow in encouraging my spouse,
please help me to remember these three ideas. I want to
make encouraging words a habit, because I know that is
pleasing to you and that it will help our relationship as a
couple to grow.*

LEARNING TO ENCOURAGE

NOT EVERYONE IS A BORN ENCOURAGER, so I want to give you some practical ideas on how to increase your word power. First, *keep it simple*. Some people feel that they must speak flowery words to be encouraging. I've sometimes called this Hallmark-itis. It's far better to use simple, straightforward words that sound like you. Your spouse will appreciate your genuine effort to express encouragement.

Second, *mean what you say*. Affirming does not mean lying or exaggerating to make your spouse feel better about himself. If you're not being sincere, you'll know it and your spouse will know it, so what's the point? Better a small compliment that is sincere than a long accolade that is all fluff.

Third, *keep the focus on your spouse, not on yourself*. If your spouse tends to reflect a compliment back to you by saying, "Oh, you're far better than I in that area," gently turn the compliment back to her. The affirmation process is not about you but about the other person.

The Bible makes it clear that believers are to encourage one another. Ephesians 4:29 gives us a significant challenge—to let everything we say be good and helpful so that others may be encouraged. Doing so with your spouse will bring optimism and blessing to your marriage.

◆ ◆ ◆

I appeal to you, dear brothers and sisters, by the authority of our Lord Jesus Christ, to live in harmony with each other. Let there be no divisions in the church. Rather, be of one mind, united in thought and purpose.

1 CORINTHIANS 1:10

Heavenly Father, I pray for wisdom and a sense of teamwork as we figure out our finances together. May we find enjoyment in the process.

HANDLING FINANCES TOGETHER

How are you handling your money? Before marriage, you probably simply bought what you wanted. But once two people merge their finances, that pattern can no longer continue. After marriage, there are two people spending money, and if both of you buy what you want, you will likely be in trouble very shortly. You don't necessarily have to ask each other every time you want to spend a dollar, but you do need a plan to make sure that you don't overspend.

Obviously, certain amounts must be set aside for the rent or house payment, utilities, gas for the car, groceries, and other bills. Also, I hope you will begin by agreeing on what you will give to God each month. But once the regular payments and gifts are set aside, you will know how much expendable money is available. Then you can decide how much to save and how much to spend. Let me share an idea: Every week, each of you should get a certain amount of money that you can use as you please. (The amount will depend upon how much discretionary money is available.) The rest of the money, you agree to spend together.

The apostle Paul reminds us that we should be "of one mind, united in thought and purpose." As couples, we need to work toward this goal in all areas of our relationship, including money. Strive toward harmony as you figure out how to spend your money. Working together on your finances can be fun and exceedingly rewarding.

◆ ◆ ◆

The plans of the diligent lead to profit as
surely as haste leads to poverty.

PROVERBS 21:5 (NIV)

Lord Jesus, it's amazing how money can slip through our fingers if we're not careful. We want to be better stewards of what you've given us. Please grant us the discipline to make and maintain a wise budget.

PLANNING YOUR FINANCES

THE WORD *BUDGET* FRIGHTENS some couples who don't want to feel tied down. The fact is, they are already on one. A budget is simply a plan for handling your money. Some people's plan is to spend it all the same day they get it. The stores stay open late to help you do that. Some people's plan is to spend it all *before* they get it. Then all you have to do is mail off payments each month. Both of these methods can bring stress to a marriage. The question is not, do you have a budget? The question is, could you have a *better* budget?

King Solomon made a wise observation in Proverbs 21:5. I don't think he was claiming that wealth is within reach for anyone who makes plans. I do think he was stating a fact of life: If you plan and make deliberate choices, the results will be better than if you simply go with the flow. That's certainly true of our finances. Planning is part of good stewardship and being wise with our resources.

If you have never put your budget on paper, I don't suggest that you do that today. Instead, keep records for two months. Record all the money you spend and what you spend it for, all the money you give away, and all the money you save. At the end of two months, you will have your budget on paper—at least, you will have a record of your budget for the past two months. Then you can examine it and ask, "Do we like our budget? If we continue with this plan, where will we be in two years?"

If you find that you don't like the way you've been allocating your money, then together you can change it. A workable budget is a genuine asset to a growing marriage.

Forgetting the past and looking forward to what lies ahead, I press on to reach the end of the race and receive the heavenly prize for which God, through Christ Jesus, is calling us.

PHILIPPIANS 3:13-14

◆

Heavenly Father, it's easy for me to waste time with things that don't really matter. But then I realize how far I am from the things that are most important. Please help us as a couple to come up with the right goals. I want to commit to doing what is best for our relationship.

SETTING GOALS FOR MARRIAGE

ONE OF THE BARRIERS TO A GROWING marriage is lack of time. One wife said, "I'd like to have a good marriage, but I'm not sure I have time." Many people can identify. After all, there are meals to be cooked, children to be reared, lawns to be mowed, and employers to be pleased. How do we find time to do all of this and still have time for each other? I'd like to share some ideas on overcoming the time barrier.

First, we must set goals. We do this in business, so why not in marriage? How often would the two of you like to go out for dinner? How often would you like to go on a weekend trip or take a walk in the park? How often would you like to experience sexual intercourse? What are the kinds of activities that would keep your marriage alive? Would you like to have a "daily sharing time" in which the two of you share your day with each other? If so, how much time would you like to invest in this? How can you pray for each other or be a spiritual encouragement to each other? These are the kinds of questions that lead to setting meaningful goals.

In Philippians 3, the apostle Paul writes about his own ultimate goal: reaching the end of the race—in other words, the end of his life of service to God—and winning the prize of God's approval. He sets aside everything else to make that his primary objective. That single-mindedness would do us good in our marriages as well. Remember, setting goals is the first step to overcoming the barrier of time, because our goals continually remind us of what's really most important.

◆ ◆ ◆

Jesus said, "Come to me, all of you who are weary and carry heavy burdens, and I will give you rest. Take my yoke upon you. Let me teach you, because I am humble and gentle at heart, and you will find rest for your souls. For my yoke is easy to bear, and the burden I give you is light."

MATTHEW 11:28-30

Father God, thank you for inviting us to come to you. I am so grateful for your forgiveness, your teaching, and your Holy Spirit, which lives in me and directs me. I need your transformation. Please help me to allow you to change me.

GOD'S POWER OF TRANSFORMATION

DOES GOD MAKE A DIFFERENCE IN MARRIAGE? Thousands of couples will testify that he made a difference in theirs. How does this transformation happen? First we must establish a relationship with God. This means that we must come to him and acknowledge that we have walked our own way and broken his laws. We tell him that we need forgiveness and we want to turn from our sins.

He stands with open arms and says, "Come to me, all of you who are weary and carry heavy burdens, and I will give you rest." That's a beautiful and astounding invitation. If we are willing to come to him, he will not only forgive us but also send his Spirit to live inside us.

The Holy Spirit is the one who changes our attitudes. When he is in control of our lives, we begin to look at things differently. He shows us that people are more important than things and that serving others is more important than being served. He works within us to produce wonderful character qualities such as love, patience, kindness, and gentleness (see Galatians 5:22-23). He alone can effect such substantial change in the way we think and act.

Do you see how these new attitudes would transform your relationship? Nothing holds greater potential for changing your marriage than asking God to come into your life, forgive your sins, and let you see the world the way he sees it.

◆ ◆ ◆

Don't worry about anything; instead, pray about everything. Tell God what you need, and thank him for all he has done. Then you will experience God's peace, which exceeds anything we can understand. . . . Fix your thoughts on what is true, and honorable, and right, and pure, and lovely, and admirable. Think about things that are excellent and worthy of praise.

PHILIPPIANS 4:6-8

Father, thank you for letting us bring anything to you in prayer. Help me to release my worries to you, knowing that you are in control. When I thank you for what you have already done, I'm reminded of how you have acted for me in the past, and I can be more positive about the future. Please encourage the right attitude in me.

MAINTAINING A POSITIVE ATTITUDE

TRYING TO KEEP A POSITIVE ATTITUDE is not a new idea. It is found clearly in the first-century writing of Paul the apostle. He encouraged the church at Philippi to pray about problems rather than worry about them. Why? Because worry leads to anxiety and negativity, while prayer leads to peace and a more positive outlook. Then Paul revealed the key to having a positive attitude: think about positive things—things that are "excellent and worthy of praise."

We are responsible for the way we think. Even in the worst marital situation, we choose our attitude. Maintaining a positive attitude requires prayer. As Paul said, we can bring our requests to God. We can tell him what we need and be thankful for what he has already done. Will God always do what we ask? No, but what does happen is that as we release worry and express gratitude, God's peace descends on our minds and hearts. God calms our emotions and directs our thoughts.

When we find ourselves struggling with an aspect of our marriage, let's try to develop a more optimistic perspective. With a positive attitude, we become a part of the solution, rather than a part of the problem.

◆ ◆ ◆

Always be joyful. Never stop praying. Be thankful in all circumstances, for this is God's will for you who belong to Christ Jesus.

1 THESSALONIANS 5:16-18

Heavenly Father, when I have a bad attitude, it comes out in the way I talk to my spouse. Please forgive me for my sharp words and negativity. I want to set a goal to avoid complaining or arguing. Instead, please help me to rejoice, pray, and be thankful. I know the resulting positive attitude will bless my spouse and strengthen our marriage.

ATTITUDE INFLUENCES BEHAVIOR

ONE REASON MY ATTITUDES ARE SO important is that they affect my actions—that is, my behavior and words. If I have a pessimistic, defeatist, negative attitude, it will be expressed in negative words and behavior. The reality is that I may not be able to control my environment. Perhaps I have experienced such difficulties as sickness, an alcoholic spouse, a teenager on drugs, a mother who abandoned me, a father who abused me, a spouse who is irresponsible, aging parents, and so on. Any one of those situations can be overwhelming. But it's crucial to realize that *I am* responsible for *what I do* within my environment. And my attitude will greatly influence my behavior.

First Thessalonians 5 gives us some key steps to developing a positive attitude: be joyful, keep praying, and be thankful in all circumstances. As we talked about in yesterday's reading, being thankful can renew our perspective, reminding us of what God has already done for us and encouraging us that he will help in the future.

If you want to know your attitude, look at your words and behavior. If your words are critical and negative, then you have a negative attitude. If your behavior is designed to hurt or get back at your spouse, then you have a negative attitude. Paul gives straightforward counsel in Philippians 2:14: "Do everything without complaining and arguing." Following this advice and guarding your attitude are the most powerful things you can do to affect your behavior. And your behavior greatly influences your marriage.

◆ ◆ ◆

If my people who are called by my name will humble themselves and pray and seek my face and turn from their wicked ways, I will hear from heaven and will forgive their sins and restore their land.

2 CHRONICLES 7:14

◆

Lord, I am amazed that you so often invite us to pray—to communicate with you, the Lord of the universe! I am grateful for the love and guidance you offer. Please help my spouse and me to take the time to pray together. May we "come boldly" to you and through our prayers be brought closer to each other and closer to you.

WHY PRAY?

BIBLE PROFESSOR HAROLD LINDSELL once said, "Why should we expect God to do *without* prayer what he has promised to do *if* we pray?" The Bible contains many calls to prayer, including God's words to Solomon, as recorded in 2 Chronicles 7. *If* the people humbled themselves and prayed after they sinned, God would hear them, forgive them, and restore them. His invitation to us is clear: "Ask me and I will tell you remarkable secrets you do not know about things to come" (Jeremiah 33:3). The author of Hebrews tells us to "come boldly" to God's throne, where we will receive mercy and grace (4:16).

We come to God as our Father, knowing that he wants to do good things for his children. But we must be ready to receive them. Thus, he says, "keep on asking, and you will receive what you ask for" (Matthew 7:7). Now, granted, God does not do everything that we request. He loves us too much and is too wise to do that. If what we request is not for our ultimate good, then he will do something better. His will is always right.

Couples who learn to pray together are simply responding to God's invitation. He wants to be involved in your marriage. Praying together is one way of acknowledging that you want his presence and his power. Through prayer, he can change your attitudes and your behavior. Remember, God is love, and he can teach you how to love each other. "Keep on asking."

◆ ◆ ◆

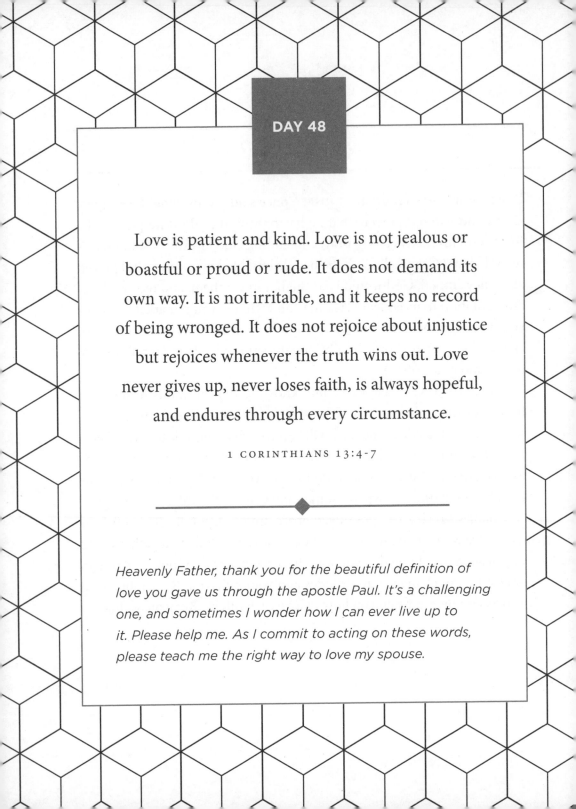

DAY 48

Love is patient and kind. Love is not jealous or boastful or proud or rude. It does not demand its own way. It is not irritable, and it keeps no record of being wronged. It does not rejoice about injustice but rejoices whenever the truth wins out. Love never gives up, never loses faith, is always hopeful, and endures through every circumstance.

1 CORINTHIANS 13:4-7

Heavenly Father, thank you for the beautiful definition of love you gave us through the apostle Paul. It's a challenging one, and sometimes I wonder how I can ever live up to it. Please help me. As I commit to acting on these words, please teach me the right way to love my spouse.

REDISCOVERING LOVE

COUPLES OFTEN COME TO ME in the midst of marriage difficulty, even at the point of separating. When I ask why they are considering such a step, they share their points of contention and conclude with the statement "We just don't love each other anymore." That is supposed to settle it. They say they have simply "lost" their love, and it's beyond their control. I don't believe that. I'll agree that they may have lost their warm romantic feelings, but real love is another matter.

The Bible makes some strong statements about love within marriage. In Ephesians 5:25, husbands are *commanded* to love their wives. In Titus 2:4, wives are told that they must *learn to love* their husbands. Anything that can be commanded, and anything that can be taught and learned, is not beyond our control.

First Corinthians 13 describes love as being patient and kind, not arrogant or rude. It describes love as refusing to keep a score of wrongs and never holding on to grudges. These words are not describing a feeling. Rather, they are talking about the way we think and behave. We can love each other without having the "tingles" for each other. In fact, the fastest way to see our emotions return is to start loving each other by acting in accordance with today's passage from 1 Corinthians 13.

◆ ◆ ◆

DAY 49

Some people make cutting remarks,
but the words of the wise bring healing.
Truthful words stand the test of time.

PROVERBS 12:18-19

◆

Lord Jesus, help me to remember that my words are powerful. I want to use them to build up and give life, not to cut down and bring discouragement. Please help me to use my words today to express love to my spouse.

LOVING THROUGH WORDS

THERE ARE TWO BASIC WAYS to express love in a marriage: *words* and *deeds*. Today, we'll look at words. First Corinthians 8:1 says, "Love edifies" (NKJV) or "builds up" (NIV). So if I want to love, I will use words that build up my spouse. "You look nice in that outfit." "Thanks for taking the garbage out." "I loved the meal. Thanks for all your hard work." "I appreciate your walking the dog for me Tuesday night. It was a real help." All of these are expressions of love.

Proverbs 18:21 tells us, "Death and life are in the power of the tongue" (NKJV). Words are powerful. You can kill your spouse's spirit with negative words—words that belittle, disrespect, or embarrass. You can give life with positive words—words that encourage, affirm, or strengthen. I met a woman some time ago who complained that she couldn't think of anything good to say about her husband. I asked, "Does he ever take a shower?" "Yes," she replied. "Then I'd start there," I said. "There are men who don't."

I've never met a person about whom you couldn't find something good to say. And when you say it, something inside the person wants to be better. Say something kind and life giving to your spouse today and see what happens.

◆ ◆ ◆

Dear children, let's not merely say that we love each other; let us show the truth by our actions.

1 JOHN 3:18

◆

Lord, I know that both words and actions are important. Please help me to express my love through the things I say and do. I want to show my spouse how sincere my love is.

LOVING THROUGH DEEDS

IN YESTERDAY'S READING, I suggested there are two basic ways to express love to your spouse: through *words* and through *deeds*. Today we'll look at deeds. As we see today's verse, the apostle John wrote that we should show our love for each other through actions, not just words. It can be easy to speak words, but our sincerity is proved through what we do. *Do something to show your love.*

Love is kind, the Bible says (see 1 Corinthians 13:4). So to express your love, find something kind and do it. It might be giving him an unexpected gift or washing the car that he drives. It might be offering to stay home with the children while she goes shopping or hiking. Or perhaps it's picking up dinner on the way home when you know she's had a hectic day. How long has it been since you wrote your spouse a love letter?

Love is patient (see 1 Corinthians 13:4). So stop pacing the floor while your spouse is getting ready to go. Sit down, relax, read your Bible, and pray. Love is also courteous. Another way to say it might be *courtly*. So do some of the things you did when you were courting. Reach over and touch his knee or take her hand. Open the door for her. Say please and thank you. Be polite. Express your love by your actions.

◆ ◆ ◆

Our bodies have many parts, and God has put each part just where he wants it. How strange a body would be if it had only one part! Yes, there are many parts, but only one body. The eye can never say to the hand, "I don't need you." The head can't say to the feet, "I don't need you."

1 CORINTHIANS 12:18-21

Father, please give me the humility to realize that I can learn from my spouse. Help me to look at our differences as opportunities to grow, not as frustrations. Thank you for making us so different, yet preparing us to fit together perfectly.

LEARNING FROM DIFFERENCES

HAVE YOU EVER THANKED GOD that you and your spouse are very different? Most of the time, we see our differences as irritations. Nathan is by nature a couch potato. His wife, Ashley, is always doing something. In the past, she viewed Nathan as lazy; he viewed her as so nervous she couldn't relax. They often had words over this difference, but most of the time they simply lived with a low-grade resentment toward each other.

Once they discovered that differences were meant to be a blessing and not a curse, they each thanked God for the other. The next step was to ask, "What can we learn from each other?" Ashley learned how to relax and watch a TV show without jumping up to do something else at the same time. Nathan learned to help with the housework, so Ashley could have time to relax and not feel guilty. Together they enriched each other's life.

That is what marriage is all about. We are trying to learn how to make the best of our differences. Again, the Bible is clear that the body of Christ benefits from many different people working together. In the church as well as in marriage, we need each other. We can't function without diversity, and that knowledge should lead us to thank God for the differences. Once you've done that, ask him to show each of you what you can learn from the other. You may be surprised at God's answer.

◆ ◆ ◆

As the deer longs for streams of water, so I long for you, O God. I thirst for God, the living God. When can I go and stand before him?

PSALM 42:1-2

Father, I want to long for you as a deer longs for water. And in the same way, I desire a deeper connection with my spouse. Please help me to remember that connection and oneness come with time and effort. Please bless our efforts to set aside time for each other.

BECOMING ONE

AFTER THE CREATION OF ADAM AND EVE, God said that the two should become one. Becoming "one" does not mean that we lose our personal identities. We retain our personalities, and we still have personal goals and ambitions. We each have our own pursuits; the typical husband and wife spend many hours each day geographically separated from each other. Marital "oneness" is not sameness. It is rather that inner feeling that assures us that we are "together" even when we are apart.

Such oneness is not automatic. Becoming "one" is the result of many shared thoughts, feelings, activities, dreams, frustrations, joys, and sorrows. In short, it is the result of sharing life.

Many couples have found that the secret to growing in oneness is establishing a daily sharing time. Many people have a daily "quiet time" with God for the purpose of getting close to him. As the author of Psalm 42 conveys so beautifully, when we're strong in our relationship with God, we long for him and desire to be near him. It's a bit circular. When we know God, we desire to spend time with him. If we spend time with him, we begin to desire him more. The same thing can be true with our spouse. The more we set aside time to spend together, the more important it becomes to us.

I encourage you to consider having a daily sharing time with your spouse for the purpose of staying close to each other. Set aside time each day to talk and to share your thoughts, emotions, and concerns. Conversation leads to understanding and unity.

Two people are better off than one, for they can help each other succeed. If one person falls, the other can reach out and help. But someone who falls alone is in real trouble.

ECCLESIASTES 4:9-10

Father, you know how lonely I feel sometimes. Thank you for giving me my spouse, and thank you for creating us to be companions who can help each other and relieve each other's loneliness. Please give us the courage to take those first steps toward closer companionship.

SEEKING COMPANIONSHIP

MARRIAGE WAS DESIGNED BY GOD to meet man's need for companionship. God said of Adam, "It is not good for the man to be alone. I will make a helper who is just right for him" (Genesis 2:18). However, some couples have not found companionship in marriage. They are still alone, cut off, and isolated.

Such loneliness may be painful, but it is doesn't have to last forever. We can overcome loneliness by taking positive action. I suggest taking "baby steps." Don't look at the whole and think about how bad your marriage is. Rather, focus on one step you might take to make it better.

Break through the silence with one act of kindness. Give her a flower, and say, "I was thinking about you today." Look for something he does well and tell him you appreciate it. Give him a passionate kiss, and say, "I just wanted to remind you of what it was like when we first married. I'm willing to start over if you are." Remember that the Bible is clear about the benefits of companionship, as we read in the book of Ecclesiastes. We are made for each other, and we can support each other in innumerable ways. Keep taking steps toward each other, and loneliness will evaporate.

◆ ◆ ◆

"You will seek me and find me when you seek me
with all your heart. I will be found by you,"
declares the LORD.

JEREMIAH 29:13-14 (NIV)

Heavenly Father, I'm so grateful for your promise that when we seek you wholeheartedly, we will find you. Please help me to devote the same kind of effort to "seeking" and knowing my spouse. Show me how to listen carefully to his or her thoughts and to value them. May this strengthen our relationship.

BUILDING INTIMACY THROUGH LISTENING

WHAT ARE THE REWARDS of listening to your spouse? Listening is the doorway into your spouse's heart and mind. God told Israel, "I know the plans I have for you. . . . They are plans for good and not for disaster, to give you a future and a hope" (Jeremiah 29:11). But how was Israel to know what was on God's heart and in God's mind? Verses 13 and 14 make it clear that they would discover the Lord when they sought him wholeheartedly. God wanted Israel to know his thoughts, but Israel had to listen.

What are you doing to seek to know the thoughts and feelings of your spouse? Listening is the key to good communication. Don't condemn your spouse for not talking more. Rather, ask questions, and then listen to the answers. They may be short at first, especially if your spouse is not the talkative type. But once your spouse realizes that you are truly interested, she will eventually share her thoughts. Accept your spouse's thoughts as interesting, challenging, or fascinating, and he will talk more.

Listening to God brings you close to his heart. Listening to your spouse brings you the same kind of intimacy.

◆ ◆ ◆

[Jesus said,] "To those who listen to my teaching, more understanding will be given, and they will have an abundance of knowledge."

MATTHEW 13:12

◆

Lord, I want to listen well to my spouse and gain more and more understanding of this person I love. I know that needs to start with valuing the times when he or she shares thoughts and feelings with me. Please give me the self-discipline to be an active, alert listener so our communication will be stronger and stronger.

CAREFUL LISTENING

YOU CANNOT OVERESTIMATE the importance of listening to your spouse. Listening says, "I value you and our relationship. I want to know you." You can never have an intimate marriage if you don't know your spouse.

Respecting the other person's ideas, even when they differ from your own, is essential to communication. Few people will continue to communicate if their thoughts are always condemned. Also, responding too quickly gets in the way of effective listening. Listen twice as much as you talk, and you will know your spouse much better. Jesus told his disciples in Matthew 13:12 that listening brings knowledge. The more we listen and the better we listen, the more we understand. That's certainly true of Jesus' teachings, but it also applies to conversations with our spouse.

If your spouse starts talking, take it as a "holy moment." The one you love is about to reveal something. When your spouse begins to reveal his or her inner self, don't do anything to stop the flow. Drop everything else and focus on listening. Nod sympathetically. Smile if your spouse says something funny. Let your eyes show concern if your spouse expresses pain. Ask questions to make sure you're getting the message. Good, active listening stimulates communication.

◆ ◆ ◆

Who can find a virtuous and capable wife? She is more precious than rubies. Her husband can trust her, and she will greatly enrich his life. She brings him good, not harm, all the days of her life. . . . When she speaks, her words are wise, and she gives instructions with kindness.

PROVERBS 31:10-12, 26

◆

Heavenly Father, please forgive me for the wrong things I have done in my marriage. I sometimes get frustrated with my husband's actions, but I forget that I contribute to the problems in our relationship as well. Please help me to admit my part and start by changing myself. May I bring good to my husband.

WISDOM FOR WIVES

WHAT'S A WIFE TO DO when her husband refuses to get with the program? You've asked him again and again to change. You've told him exactly what you want, but he doesn't budge. So, what are you to do?

Let me suggest that you take a different approach. Since he isn't changing, start with yourself. Look carefully at your own behavior and ask yourself, *What have I been doing that I should not be doing? What have I been saying that I should not be saying?* Your answers may include trying to control him, speaking unkindly, or harboring bitterness. Once you've identified them, confess these things to God and then to your husband. Even if your husband is 95 percent of the problem, the place for you to start is with your 5 percent. After all, you *can* change that, and when you do, your marriage will be 5 percent better.

Consider this approach from a wife who tends to treat her husband like hired help: "It was unfair of me to ask you to get rid of that tree stump right after you mowed the lawn. I know I've piled tasks on you before, and I'm sorry. I want you to know that I appreciate the work you did this morning." Whatever his initial response, she has just changed the climate of her marriage.

Strive to be a wife who, like the famous "Proverbs 31 woman," speaks wisely and kindly, and brings good to her husband.

◆ ◆ ◆

Husbands ought to love their wives as they love their own bodies. For a man who loves his wife actually shows love for himself.

EPHESIANS 5:28

Father, loving my wife as I love my own body is a huge challenge that sometimes seems insurmountable. I want to learn more about how to do that. Please help me grow in the way I treat my wife, so that our marriage may become stronger and more intimate.

WISDOM FOR HUSBANDS

WANT TO HAVE A MORE LOVING WIFE? Before criticizing her for all her faults, remember that criticism rarely works to bring about positive change. But here are some ideas that *will* work.

First, find something you like about her and express your appreciation. Do it again two days later, and then do it again. When you develop a pattern of compliments, you may be pleasantly surprised with the results.

Second, speak kindly. Don't allow your emotions to dictate your tone of voice. If you have something to say, even if it involves negative feelings, say it as kindly as possible. Remember that the Bible says, "A gentle answer deflects anger, but harsh words make tempers flare" (Proverbs 15:1). Don't stir up anger unnecessarily.

Third, don't give orders. Demands create resentment. Instead of saying, "I want this done today," try asking, "Is there any chance that you could work this into your schedule today? I'd really appreciate it if you can." The way you talk to your wife makes all the difference in the world.

Above all, remember that your responsibility is to love your wife as you love your own body. That means caring for her and treating her respectfully, no matter how she acts or how she responds to you. Let love be your goal, and everything else will fall into place.

◆ ◆ ◆

Whenever we have the opportunity, we should do
good to everyone—especially to those in
the family of faith.

GALATIANS 6:10

*Father, there are so many ways to show my love through
acts of service. Please help me to notice the opportunities
throughout the day.*

SHOWING LOVE THROUGH SERVICE

FOR SOME PEOPLE, actions speak louder than words. Acts of service is probably the primary love language of these people. It's what makes them feel loved. The words "I love you" may seem shallow to these folks if they are not accompanied by acts of service.

Mowing the grass, cooking a meal, washing dishes, vacuuming the floor, getting hairs out of the sink, removing the white spots from the mirror, getting bugs off the windshield, taking out the garbage, changing the baby's diaper, painting the bedroom, dusting the bookcase, washing the car, trimming the shrubs, raking the leaves, dusting the blinds, walking the dog—these types of things communicate love to the person whose primary love language is acts of service. In Galatians, Paul encourages us to take opportunities to do good and kind things for other believers. How much more should we do this for the one we love most?

Do these things, and your spouse will feel loved. Fail to do these things, and you can say, "I love you" all day long without making him or her feel loved. If you want your spouse to feel loved, you must discover and speak his or her primary love language.

◆ ◆ ◆

Live a life filled with love, following the example of Christ. He loved us and offered himself as a sacrifice for us, a pleasing aroma to God.

EPHESIANS 5:2

Lord, I want to please you through my acts of love and service to my husband or wife. Help me to focus my energies on him or her, not on myself. Enrich our marriage through expressions of love.

COMMUNICATING LOVE

WHAT WOULD YOU LIKE your spouse to do for you? Your answer to this question will probably reveal your primary love language. If your answer is clean out the garage, paint the bedroom, vacuum the floors, wash dishes, or walk the dog, then your primary love language is acts of service. If you would really like your spouse to hold your hand when you go for a walk, your primary love language is probably physical touch. When you know which of the five love languages most connects with you and your spouse, you know what needs to happen to really make both of you feel loved.

Before you start preaching to your spouse about speaking your love language, stop and ask yourself, "Does my spouse feel loved by me?" You might even ask your spouse, "On a scale of 0 to 10, how full is your love tank? That is, how much do you feel loved by me?" If the answer is anything less than 10, ask, "What could I do to help fill it?" Whatever your spouse suggests, do it to the best of your ability. After all, in Ephesians 5, Paul challenges us to "live a life filled with love." When we follow Christ's example and offer love freely to each other, good things happen. As you learn to speak your spouse's love language, chances are, your spouse will learn to speak yours.

◆ ◆ ◆

Let love be your highest goal!

1 CORINTHIANS 14:1

Lord Jesus, help me to make love my highest goal—both in life and in my marriage. Please give me wisdom as I observe my spouse and try to figure out his or her love language. I want to love him or her well.

EXPRESSING LOVE

WOULD YOU LIKE TO KNOW your spouse's love language? Then observe how he or she most often expresses love to you. Is it through words of affirmation? Gifts? Acts of service? Quality time? Or physical touch? The way a person expresses love to you is likely the way he or she wishes you would express your love.

If he often hugs and kisses you, his love language is probably *physical touch*. He wishes you would take initiative to hug and kiss him. If she is always weeding the flower beds, keeping the finances in order, or cleaning up the bathroom after you leave, then her love language is probably *acts of service*. She wishes that you would help her with the work around the house. If you don't, then she feels unloved. One husband said, "If I had known that my taking out the garbage would make her feel loved and more responsive sexually, I would have started taking out the garbage years ago." Too bad it took him so many years to learn his wife's primary love language. As the Bible says, love should be our highest goal. To reach that goal, we need to put forth an effort to know how our spouse can best receive love.

◆ ◆ ◆

Love never gives up, never loses faith, is always hopeful, and endures through every circumstance.

1 CORINTHIANS 13:7

Father, I want our relationship as a couple to grow. Please help me to discover my spouse's love language, and show me how to speak it effectively.

FINDING THE GOOD IN COMPLAINTS

WHAT DOES YOUR SPOUSE COMPLAIN about most often? We usually interpret complaints as negative criticism, but they actually give us valuable information. Complaints reveal the heart. A person's recurring complaint often reveals his or her love language.

If a husband frequently says, "We don't ever spend time together. We're like two ships passing in the night," he is telling his wife that *quality time* is his primary love language and his love tank is sitting on empty.

If a wife says, "I don't think you would ever touch me if I didn't initiate it," she is revealing that *physical touch* is her love language.

If a husband returns from a business trip and his wife says, "You mean you didn't bring me anything?" she is telling him that *gifts* is her love language. She can't believe that he came home empty-handed.

If a wife complains, "I don't ever do anything right," she is saying that *words of affirmation* is her love language, and she is not hearing those words.

If a husband says, "If you loved me, you would help me," he is shouting that his love language is *acts of service*.

Do you feel frustrated because you don't seem to be communicating love to your spouse? First Corinthians 13 reminds us never to give up. Things can improve when we maintain hope. Discovering and speaking your spouse's love language is one way to help your relationship grow.

◆ ◆ ◆

Encourage one another daily, as long as it is called "Today," so that none of you may be hardened by sin's deceitfulness.

HEBREWS 3:13 (NIV)

Father, I don't want my spouse's heart to be hardened by my negativity. Please help me to encourage through my loving, encouraging words. I see so much in my loved one that is good, and I need to say so. Thank you for affirming me through the loving words I read in the Bible.

CHANGE THROUGH AFFIRMATION

WHAT WOULD LIFE BE LIKE if your spouse gave you encouraging words every day? "Like heaven," one husband said. One woman responded, "I'd think my husband was drunk." How tragic that we typically give each other so few words of affirmation. We allow the emotions of hurt, disappointment, and anger to keep us from speaking positive words to each other, or maybe we simply get stuck in a pattern of negative comments. As a result, distance and dissatisfaction grow.

All of us long to hear affirming words, and those whose primary love language is affirming words long for them even more. We like to sense that our efforts are appreciated, and that our spouse sees something good in us. When we are affirmed, we aspire to be better. When we are ignored or condemned, we either become discouraged and withdraw, or become angry and hostile. Positive words can change the emotional atmosphere in a marriage. We need to look for something good in our spouse and affirm it.

The apostle Paul challenged his readers to "encourage each another and build each other up" (1 Thessalonians 5:11). The author of Hebrews suggested that believers give each other daily encouragement as a safeguard against hardened hearts and sin. Encouragement is important. Our words are like medication to a sick relationship. There is healing, and it often begins with words of affirmation.

◆ ◆ ◆

I commend to you our sister Phoebe, who is a deacon in the church in Cenchrea. Welcome her in the Lord as one who is worthy of honor among God's people. Help her in whatever she needs, for she has been helpful to many, and especially to me.

ROMANS 16:1-2

◆

Lord Jesus, I pray that you would help me to think before I respond to my spouse. Show me how best to be an encouragement. I don't want to stand in the way of my loved one's goals, so please help me develop a pattern of encouragement and specific affirmation. I know that will strengthen our relationship.

ENCOURAGING SUCCESS

ENCOURAGING WORDS OFTEN MAKE the difference between success and failure. For example, imagine that your spouse expresses the desire to lose weight. How you respond can be either encouraging or discouraging. If you say, "Well, I hope you don't try one of those expensive weight-loss programs or join a pricey gym. We can't afford that," then you have discouraged your spouse. Chances are, he or she will drop the idea and make no effort to lose weight.

On the other hand, consider this response: "Well, one thing I know. If you decide to lose weight, you will, because you have the discipline to do it. That's one of the things I admire about you." Wow! Your spouse is encouraged and will likely take action immediately.

At the end of the book of Romans, Paul writes a number of personal greetings, many of them including affirmations. In today's verses, he mentions a woman named Phoebe, who is "worthy of honor" and "helpful." Later in the chapter, he mentions several others by name and lists their contribution to his work. Imagine being praised in Paul's letter! The specifics he included give impact to his encouraging words.

When you have a chance to respond to your spouse, think before you speak. Ask yourself, *What can I say that would affirm and encourage my spouse to reach his or her goals?* Most of us are motivated when we hear encouraging words.

◆ ◆ ◆

A gentle answer deflects anger,
but harsh words make tempers flare.

PROVERBS 15:1

Dear Lord, I want to affirm my spouse by the things I say as well as the way I say them. Please help me to remember that kindness will always go further than criticism. Guard me from yelling or screaming at my spouse; please show me the way to speak with gentleness and kindness.

GENTLE WORDS

POSITIVE WORDS ARE POWERFUL TOOLS in building a strong marriage. When my wife compliments me on something, it makes me want to do more. When she criticizes me, it makes me want to defend myself and fight back. If you want to see your spouse blossom, try giving a compliment every day for thirty days and see what happens.

Have you ever noticed that when you speak softly, your spouse seems to calm down, and when you speak harshly, your spouse tends to get louder? We influence each other not only by what we say, but by how we say it. Screaming is a learned behavior, and it can be unlearned. We don't have to yell at each other. The above verse from Proverbs tells us what we instinctively know: Harsh words lead to more anger, but gentle words can defuse the situation. It's all in how we say it.

If you have a problem that you need to discuss with your spouse, write out what you want to say. Stand in front of a mirror and make your presentation in a soft voice. Then ask God to help you use the same tone of voice when you talk to your spouse. You may not be perfect the first time, but you will learn to speak the truth in love and gentleness.

◆ ◆ ◆

Wise words satisfy like a good meal; the right words bring satisfaction. The tongue can bring death or life.

PROVERBS 18:20-21

Heavenly Father, thank you for the gift of encouragement. I want to be an encourager in my marriage; I want to bring satisfaction and hope with what I say, rather than discouragement or frustration. Please help me as I try to develop the habit of sharing positive words.

ENCOURAGING WORDS

THIS PROVERB IS TRUE: "The tongue can bring death or life." You can kill your spouse's spirit with negative words, and you can give life through positive words. Encouraging words should be the norm in your marriage. You can't treat encouragement like a fire extinguisher, pulling it out only when you really need it and then putting it away again. Encouragement needs to be a way of life.

Encouraging words grow out of an attitude of kindness. When I choose to be kind to my spouse, to look for her positive qualities, and to do things that will make her life easier, then positive words begin to show up in my vocabulary. Complaining, cutting remarks grow out of a negative attitude. If I focus on the worst in my spouse and think about what she should be doing for me, then I become negative. I will destroy my spouse with my negative words.

I encourage you to give your spouse life by choosing positive, affirming words. The Bible tells us that wise or helpful words bring satisfaction. Proverbs 20:15 compares the value of wise words to gold and many rubies. Encouragement can work wonders in a relationship. Look for something good in your spouse and express your appreciation. Do it today—and every day.

◆ ◆ ◆

"Let [Rebekah] be the wife of your master's son, as the LORD has directed." When Abraham's servant heard their answer, he bowed down to the ground and worshiped the LORD. Then he brought out silver and gold jewelry and clothing and presented them to Rebekah. He also gave expensive presents to her brother and mother.

GENESIS 24:51-53

Lord God, sometimes I forget how much a small gesture can mean to my spouse—even if his or her primary love language isn't gifts. Please help me to be thoughtful and to show him or her how much I care.

SPEAKING LOVE THROUGH GIFTS

My ACADEMIC BACKGROUND is anthropology. In all the cultures around the world that anthropologists have studied, they have never discovered a culture where gift giving is not a part of the love and marriage process. The biblical account of Rebekah's engagement to Isaac clearly shows this custom. Once she and her family had agreed that she would be Isaac's wife, Abraham's servant gave her costly gifts to show his master's sincerity and respect. Giving gifts as an expression of love is universal. A gift is a visible token that says, "I was thinking about you."

Receiving gifts is some people's primary love language. Nothing speaks louder of a spouse's devotion. Unfortunately, these people are often married to others who don't speak this love language very well.

A man may have given gifts before marriage because he thought that was a part of courtship, but after marriage the gift giving stopped. Perhaps he expresses love in other ways, but he ceases to give gifts. I remember the wife who said, "My husband tells me that he loves me, but to me, words are cheap. 'I love you. I love you.' I'm sick of words. Where are the gifts?" Her husband's words may be sincere, but he's speaking the wrong love language. For his wife, one gift is worth a thousand words.

If that's true of your spouse as well, make sure you're finding an appropriate way to express your love.

◆ ◆ ◆

When [the wise men] saw the star, they were filled with joy! They entered the house and saw the child with his mother, Mary, and they bowed down and worshiped him. Then they opened their treasure chests and gave him gifts of gold, frankincense, and myrrh.

MATTHEW 2:10-11

Father, thank you for the example of the wise men, who brought the best they had to show their love for Jesus. Help me to do my best to express love to my spouse through thoughtful, meaningful gifts.

EVIDENCE OF LOVE

WHEN IS THE LAST TIME YOU GAVE your spouse a gift? What did you give? If you can't answer those questions, a gift is long overdue. Gift giving is one of the five fundamental languages of love. A gift to your spouse is visible evidence of your loving thoughts.

The most famous gifts in the Bible are undoubtedly the gifts from the wise men to the baby Jesus. These men brought costly gifts of gold and expensive spices, and in doing so they honored Jesus and showed that they believed him to be a king. I'm sure Mary and Joseph were awed by these beautiful things and the love for their son they signified.

The gift need not be expensive. Guys, you can get flowers free. Just go out in your yard and pick them. That's what your children do. No flowers in your yard? Try your neighbors' yard. Ask them; they'll give you a few flowers.

However, if you can afford to buy gifts, don't give free flowers. Why not invest some of your money in your marriage? Give your spouse something you know will be appreciated. If you're not certain, ask! Explain that you want to do something nice, and ask for a list of some things your spouse would like to have. That's valuable information. Use it to build your relationship.

◆ ◆ ◆

O God, you are my God; I earnestly search for you.
My soul thirsts for you; my whole body longs for
you in this parched and weary land where
there is no water.

PSALM 63:1

◆

*Father, you know how much I need you—and how much
I need my spouse. Time with him or her refreshes me,
connects us, and shows that I care. Please help us to make
this a priority as a couple.*

MAKING ROOM FOR QUALITY TIME

HOW MUCH TIME DO YOU SPEND with your spouse each day? Chances are, you are apart more than you are together, if you don't count the time you are asleep. That's pretty normal. One or both of you are likely working, and normally we don't work at the same place.

When you are together, how much time do you spend actually talking with each other? One hour a day? Probably not. Most couples spend less than thirty minutes each day in conversation. Much of this is spent on logistics, like, "What time am I supposed to pick up Jordan from soccer practice?" When do you have quality conversation, where you talk about issues, desires, frustrations, and joys?

Why not start with fifteen minutes a day? Call it couple time, talk time, or couch time. What you call it is not important. What is important is that the two of you spend quality time each day talking and listening to each other. Not only do you exchange information, but you communicate that you care about each other.

As believers, we may make time with God a priority but not time with our spouse. When King David wrote Psalm 63, he vividly expressed his longing for time and communication with the Lord, comparing it to water in a dry and weary place. Time with God refreshes us spiritually, and quality time with our spouse refreshes us emotionally and relationally. Quality time sends a strong emotional message: "I think you're important. I enjoy being with you. Let's do this again tomorrow."

◆ ◆ ◆

Love each other with genuine affection, and take delight in honoring each other.

ROMANS 12:10

◆

Lord God, please help me to be aware of my spouse's love language. Show me how I can effectively communicate love to him or her. Help me to make quality time a priority for both of us.

COMMUNICATING LOVE
THROUGH QUALITY TIME

QUALITY TIME IS ONE OF THE FIVE basic languages of love. It is some people's primary love language, and nothing else makes them feel more loved. What is quality time? It's giving your spouse your undivided attention. More than simply being in the same room, it's making eye contact, talking and listening sympathetically, or doing something together. *What you do is not so important.* Your focus is on being with each other, not on the activity.

How long has it been since you planned a weekend getaway? If that seems overwhelming, maybe you should start with a night out. Or how about just twenty minutes on the couch talking to each other? Better yet, ask your spouse what he or she would like to do.

If quality time is your spouse's primary love language and you haven't been speaking that language, chances are he or she has been complaining. You might hear, "We don't ever spend any time together. We used to take walks, but we haven't taken a walk together in two years." Some might even say, "I feel like you don't love me." Rather than getting defensive, why not recognize the problem and respond positively? Remember, the Bible tells us to love each other genuinely and to "take delight" in pleasing and honoring each other. Say, "You're right, honey. Why don't we take a walk tonight?"

◆ ◆ ◆

Imitate God, therefore, in everything you do, because you are his dear children. Live a life filled with love, following the example of Christ. He loved us and offered himself as a sacrifice for us, a pleasing aroma to God.

EPHESIANS 5:1-2

♦

Father, thank you for the transforming power of love. Your love for me gives me so many things—self-worth, purpose, and eternal life. May I learn to imitate you in the way I love my spouse, and may that love lead to greater unity.

THE POWER OF LOVE

IN THE CONTEXT OF MARRIAGE, if we do not feel loved, our differences are magnified. We each come to view the other as a threat to our happiness. We fight for self-worth and significance, and marriage becomes a battlefield rather than a haven.

Love is not the answer to every problem, but it creates a climate of security in which we can seek answers to those issues that bother us. In the security of love, a couple can discuss differences without fear of condemnation. Conflicts can be resolved. Two people who are different can learn to live together in harmony and discover how to bring out the best in each other. Those are the rewards of love.

Love really is the most powerful force in the world. It was love that led Christ to give his life for us. We have eternal life because of his love, and we also have an opportunity to love each other as his representatives. In Ephesians 5, the apostle Paul encourages us to follow Christ's example and live a life of love. Marriages function best when both partners feel genuinely loved. The decision to love your spouse holds tremendous potential. Learning his or her primary love language makes that potential a reality.

◆ ◆ ◆

Husbands, live with your wives in an
understanding way.

1 PETER 3:7 (ESV)

◆

*Father, thank you for the gift of physical touch. I want
to use it to communicate my love. Please help me to be
attuned to my spouse's needs and desires, not just my own.*

DIALECT OF TOUCH

IN MARRIAGE, the love language of *physical touch* has many dialects. This does not mean that all touches are created equal. Some will bring more pleasure to your spouse than others. Your best instructor is your spouse. Your wife knows what she perceives as a loving touch; don't insist on touching her in your way and in your time. Respect her wishes. Learn to speak her dialect. Don't make the mistake of believing that the touch that brings pleasure to you will also bring the most pleasure to her.

First Peter 3:7 says that husbands are to dwell with our wives "according to knowledge" (KJV) or "in an understanding way" (ESV). In other words, we need to know our spouse on a deep level. Men, the primary source of knowledge about what makes your wife feel loved is your wife. Some wives enjoy a back rub, others can take it or leave it, and others find it annoying. Women, of course the same goes for husbands.

God made your spouse unique. Physical touch is one of the five love languages, but you must discover what *kind* of touches your spouse enjoys. When you speak the right dialect of physical touch, your loved one will feel loved.

◆ ◆ ◆

Kiss me and kiss me again, for your
love is sweeter than wine.

SONG OF SONGS 1:2

---

*Dear Lord, help me to be generous with my time and
touches. I want to express my love to my spouse in more
creative ways.*

CREATIVE TOUCH

LOVE TOUCHES MAY BE EXTENDED OR BRIEF. A back rub takes time, but putting your hand on your spouse's shoulder as you pour a cup of coffee takes only a moment. Sitting close to each other on the couch as you watch your favorite television program requires no additional time, but it may loudly communicate your love.

Touching your spouse as you walk through the room where he is sitting takes only a second. Touching each other as you leave the house and again when you return may involve only a brief kiss or hug, but it may speak volumes to your spouse.

If you discover that physical touch is your spouse's primary love language, coming up with new ways and places to touch can be an exciting challenge. You may find that you can fill your spouse's emotional love tank as you stroll across the parking lot, simply by holding hands. A kiss after you get in the car might make the drive home much shorter. Solomon's book Song of Songs is a description of a husband and wife taking joy in touching each other. It can be inspiring reading if you're trying to think of new ways to express love to your spouse through physical touch.

◆ ◆ ◆

If only someone would listen to me!
Look, I will sign my name to my defense.

JOB 31:35

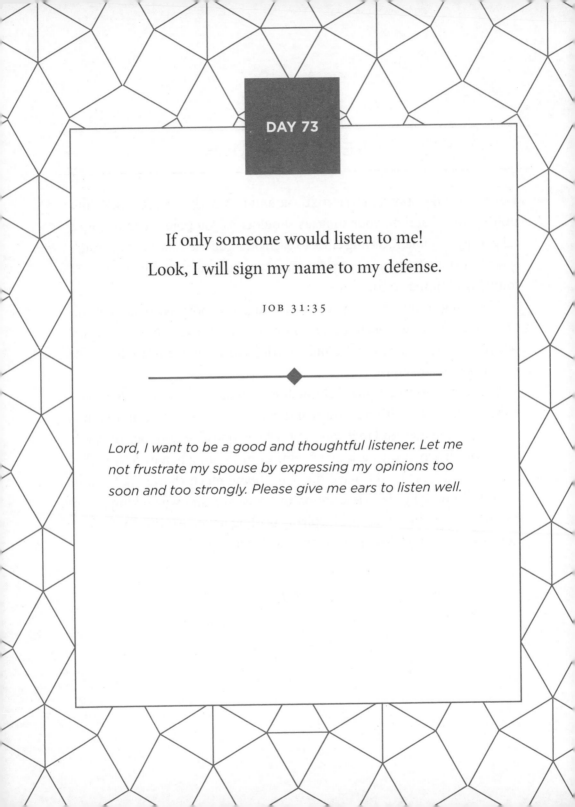

Lord, I want to be a good and thoughtful listener. Let me not frustrate my spouse by expressing my opinions too soon and too strongly. Please give me ears to listen well.

LISTEN FIRST, THEN RESPOND

MOST OF US SHARE OUR IDEAS much too soon. We talk before we have really listened. In fact, one research project found that the average person will listen only seventeen seconds before interrupting.

The book of Job gives many illustrations of poor listening. As Job suffered with physical illness, grief, and loss of material things, he steadfastly maintained his good standing before God. But his "friends" brushed him off and stated insistently that he must have committed some great sin for God to allow him to suffer so much. Finally, after pages of speeches, Job gets fed up. We can hear his frustration in his words: "If only someone would listen to me!"

A good listener will never share his ideas until he is sure that he understands what the other person is saying. In marriage, this is extremely important. Ask questions, repeat what you think your spouse is saying, and ask, "Am I understanding you?" When your spouse says, "Yes, I think you understand what I'm saying and how I feel," then and only then are you ready to move on. You might say, "I really appreciate your being open with me. Now that I understand where you're coming from, may I share what I was thinking when I did that? I realize now that what I said was hurtful, but I want you to understand that I was not trying to hurt you." At this point, your spouse will hear your perspective, because you have first taken the time to really hear what he or she was saying.

◆ ◆ ◆

Give us today the food we need, and forgive us our sins, as we have forgiven those who sin against us. And don't let us yield to temptation, but rescue us from the evil one.

MATTHEW 6:11-13

◆

Father, I can't thank you enough for your glorious forgiveness through Christ. It's an amazing gift. Since you have done this wonderful thing for me, I know that I, too, need to forgive those who sin against me. Please help me as I strive to be better at forgiving my spouse when I need to. Thank you.

FORGIVING AS GOD FORGIVES

THERE IS A DIFFERENCE BETWEEN acceptance and forgiveness. You may *accept* many things about your spouse that you do not particularly like, such as a habit that you find annoying. In fact, such acceptance is necessary in healthy marriages. But wrong, unfair, or unjust treatment—which the Bible calls sin—cannot be accepted. Sin needs to be *forgiven*.

When a spouse continues to persist in sinning, the relationship will be strained. Ideally the wrongdoer will confess his or her failures and request forgiveness. That's the biblical model. When we choose to forgive someone, we are saying, "I will no longer hold this sin against you. I will respond to you as though it had not happened. I will continue working with you on our relationship. I love you."

But what are we to do when our spouse does not confess wrongdoing and, in fact, persists in sinful behavior? We are to release the person to God, along with our anger. Then we are free to return good for evil and thus have a positive influence on our spouse.

The challenge of Scripture is to forgive one another as God forgives us. Jesus stated this plainly when he taught his disciples what we know as the Lord's Prayer. The concept is echoed other times, including in Ephesians 4, where Paul tells his listeners to "be kind to each other, tenderhearted, forgiving one another, just as God through Christ has forgiven you" (4:32). Our goal is clear, but we may need to learn how to get there.

◆ ◆ ◆

Oh, what joy for those whose disobedience is forgiven, whose sin is put out of sight!

PSALM 32:1

◆

Father, I'm in awe of your complete forgiveness of my sins. Thank you! Please give me the humility and grace to forgive my spouse like that too.

THOROUGH FORGIVENESS

A HEALTHY MARRIAGE REQUIRES confession when we do wrong and forgiveness from the one whom we have wronged. The word *confess* means to tell or make known, to acknowledge a wrongdoing. When we confess, God forgives. The Bible describes God's forgiveness as thorough. Today's verse from Psalm 32 refers to our sin as "out of sight," while Psalm 103 uses a wonderful image of distance: "He has removed our sins as far from us as the east is from the west" (Psalm 103:12). In the book of Hebrews, we hear God's promise to forget our sins: "I will never again remember their sins and lawless deeds" (Hebrews 10:17).

When your spouse sins against you, it stimulates hurt and perhaps anger. You may feel like lashing out, but the biblical response is loving confrontation. If he or she admits the wrong, the right response is to lovingly forgive. Perhaps you are saying, "But how can I forgive when it hurts so deeply?" Remember, forgiveness is not a feeling. It is rather a promise to lift judgment. "I'm deeply hurt and angry, but I choose to forgive you" is a realistic statement. You are honest about your feelings, but you are choosing to forgive. You will no longer hold the wrong against your loved one.

◆ ◆ ◆

Give all your worries and cares to God,

for he cares about you.

1 PETER 5:7

Lord, I know that you command us to forgive others when they are repentant and ask for forgiveness. It's not optional. I want to follow your ways, but sometimes my feelings get in the way. Please help me to deal with those. Thank you for helping me to forgive my spouse.

DOES FORGIVING EQUAL FORGETTING?

THERE IS A DIFFERENCE BETWEEN forgiving and forgetting. One wife said, "I've forgiven him, but I have trouble with my feelings when I remember what he did." Forgiveness does not destroy our memory. Our brains record every event we have ever experienced, good and bad. Memory may bring back the event and the feelings of hurt and pain. But keep in mind that forgiveness is not a feeling. Rather, it is a promise to no longer hold the sin against the other person.

So, what do we do when the memory comes back and we feel the pain again? We take it to God and say, "Father God, you know what I'm remembering, and you know the pain I'm feeling, but I thank you that it is forgiven. Now help me to do something loving for my spouse today." We don't allow the memory to control our behavior. In time, the pain will diminish as we build new positive memories together as a couple. Don't be troubled by memories. As 1 Peter 5:7 reminds us, we can bring all our worries to God. He cares about us and will help us forgive.

◆ ◆ ◆

Don't look out only for your own interests, but take an interest in others, too.

PHILIPPIANS 2:4

Lord God, I pray for grace to understand my spouse better when it comes to financial decisions. Please help me to see the need behind the request. Remind me to consider my spouse's interests, not just my own, and to be selfless enough to accommodate them.

FINANCIAL HARMONY

How do we find financial harmony in marriage? There is no quick route to financial unity, but each couple can and must find a way to achieve it. The process requires talking, listening, understanding, and seeking a new way—not *my* way or *your* way, but *our* way. We must try to understand the reasons behind our partner's feelings and thoughts.

For example, say a wife wants to build up five thousand dollars in a savings account. Why is that so important to her? Possibly because it gives her emotional security. With that money safe and readily available, she knows that her children will not go hungry, no matter what emergency may arise.

Now imagine that her husband is an investor who wants to make his money work for him. He feels it's a waste of resources to keep any more than one hundred dollars in a savings account. Perhaps he feels that he is not being a good steward if he does not make wise investments. That's a worthy perspective.

Until this couple understands each other's feelings and thoughts on this issue, they will find themselves arguing over what to do. But once the husband understands the emotional impact on his wife when they only have one hundred dollars in savings, then he can stop arguing and accept her need for security.

The solution? He can use whatever is available beyond the five thousand dollars for investments. Now the argument is over, and both are having their needs met. Learning to work as a team and consider others' needs and interests, as Paul challenges us to do in Philippians 2, leads to financial harmony.

The Lord doesn't see things the way you see them.
People judge by outward appearance,
but the Lord looks at the heart.

1 SAMUEL 16:7

Father, you know the depths of the human heart. Only you understand all the different things that motivate our behavior. I ask for wisdom and insight into my spouse's actions. Please grant me the grace to respond patiently and thoughtfully, considering what needs may be behind what I see.

INSIGHT INTO UNDERLYING MOTIVES

WHAT YOU SEE IS NOT ALWAYS what you get; life is much more complex than that. Human behavior is almost always motivated by unseen needs that propel us to action. That means that you can see my behavior, but you don't know my underlying motives. After all, even I may not be conscious of my motives. All of us are moved along by these strong inner forces. If we are going to understand each other, we'll have to go beneath the surface.

What are these inner needs that affect our behavior so strongly? They fall into two categories: physical and emotional. Physical needs are easy to understand—for example, thirst, hunger, or sleep. Much of our behavior is motivated by physical needs such as these.

Emotional needs are much more difficult to identify, but they are just as powerful. For example, the need to feel loved and appreciated motivates much of our behavior. If someone gives me affirming words, if I sense that they genuinely care about me, then I am motivated to spend time with that person. That's why learning to meet your spouse's need for love is so important if you want to have a growing marriage.

When you don't understand your spouse's actions, respond patiently and humbly. Take a minute to consider the needs that might be behind the behavior. That may give you new insight into what's going on and how to respond.

◆ ◆ ◆

Spouting off before listening to the facts is both
shameful and foolish.

PROVERBS 18:13

◆

*Father, in situations like these, help me to hold my tongue.
Let me not offer my spouse the first response that comes
to my mind, which is often full of my strong opinions.
Please give me the wisdom to ask questions and invite a
deeper conversation.*

WAITING FOR THE FACTS

IF I LISTEN TO MY WIFE with a view to setting her straight, I will never understand her, and most of our conversations will end in arguments. The propensity to pass judgment is what sabotages the conversations of thousands of couples. Consider a woman who says, "I think I am going to have to quit my job." Suppose her husband responds, "You can't quit your job. We can't make it without your salary. And remember, you're the one who wanted this house with the big mortgage payment." They are either on the road to an intense argument or else they will withdraw and suffer in silence, each blaming the other.

Once again, in today's proverb, King Solomon is blunt in his appraisal of those who answer before they have all the information. He calls their behavior shameful and foolish. Not only does it lead to arguments, but it stops the process of exchanging information, and no further wisdom can be attained.

How very different things will be if the husband withholds judgment and instead responds to his wife by saying, "It sounds like you had a hard day at work, honey. Do you want to talk about it?" He has now opened up the possibility of understanding his wife. And when she feels heard and understood, together they can make a wise decision regarding her job. Withholding judgment, waiting for the facts, allows the conversation to proceed.

◆ ◆ ◆

Jesus replied, "The most important commandment is this: 'Listen, O Israel! The LORD our God is the one and only LORD. And you must love the LORD your God with all your heart, all your soul, all your mind, and all your strength.' The second is equally important: 'Love your neighbor as yourself.'"

MARK 12:29-31

Father, help me to remember that the best thing I can do—both for my relationship with you and for my marriage—is to spend time communicating with you. As I read your Word, pray, and listen, please conform me more and more to the image of Christ. I know that will spill over into the way I treat my spouse.

COMMUNICATION WITH GOD

THE FUNDAMENTAL BUILDING BLOCK in any relationship is conversation—two-way communication. I share my ideas and you listen; you share your ideas and I listen. The results? We understand each other. If we continue conversation over a period of time, we get to know each other. Why, then, is communication so difficult? Why do 86 percent of those who divorce say, "The main problem was, we got to a place where we just couldn't talk"?

I want to suggest that one problem is that we stop talking to God long before we stop talking to each other. If I'm talking with God daily, he will be influencing my thoughts and attitudes toward my spouse. God has clearly said that he wants to make me more and more like Jesus (see Romans 8:29). When I cooperate with the process, my communication with my wife flows pretty smoothly. When I get my wires crossed with God, then my attitudes toward my wife begin to deteriorate.

I don't think it's a coincidence that, in Mark 12, Jesus says the most important commandments are *loving God wholeheartedly*, and *loving others as ourselves*. When we love God and are in tune with what he wants, loving others will come naturally.

I'm convinced that many of the communication problems in marriage would fade away if we spent more time talking and listening to God.

◆ ◆ ◆

We ask God to give you complete knowledge of his
will and to give you spiritual wisdom
and understanding.

COLOSSIANS 1:9

◆

*Lord God, thank you for the privilege of bringing requests
to you. Thank you, too, for the example of Paul's prayer,
which goes beyond the logistical details of our lives to the
things that really matter—my spouse's relationship with
you. Help me to be faithful as I pray for my mate.*

PRAYING FOR YOUR SPOUSE

PRAYING FOR YOUR SPOUSE may be your greatest ministry. What could be more important? Through word and example, the Bible shows us that prayer is powerful. James 5:16 says, "The earnest prayer of a righteous person has great power and produces wonderful results." Think of all the amazing examples of intercession in the Bible. Abraham pleaded with God to spare Sodom. Moses interceded for Israel after they had built the golden calf. Daniel fasted and prayed in great humility, confessing his sins and the sins of Israel. Paul prayed that the Christians at Colosse would be filled with the knowledge of God's will. Jesus prayed that Peter's faith would not fail after he denied Christ.

How are you praying for your spouse? Perhaps you could use Colossians 1:9-14 as a place to begin. As you pray what Paul prayed for these believers—that their faith would be strengthened, and that God would equip them with endurance and patience—you will be ministering to your spouse. You may also find your heart growing more tender toward him or her.

Intercessory prayer is a service to the person you are praying for. Prayer is one of God's ordained means of accomplishing his will on earth. As he allows us to preach and teach, so he allows us to pray—and so we cooperate with him in his work. Pray for your spouse today, and watch how it affects your marriage.

◆ ◆ ◆

[Jesus said,] "Where two or three gather together as my followers, I am there among them."

MATTHEW 18:20

◆

Father, I'm grateful for your promise to be present with us when we pray together. Sometimes that feels awkward or difficult, but please help us to commit to praying together as a couple. I know it's important for us spiritually and emotionally.

PRAYING TOGETHER

MANY COUPLES FIND IT DIFFICULT to pray together. Why? One reason may be that they are not treating each other with love and respect, and that stands as a barrier between them. The answer to this problem is confession and repentance. First John 1:9 says, "If we confess our sins to him, he is faithful and just to forgive us our sins." It is a sin to fail to love your spouse, or to fail to treat him or her with kindness and respect. Such sin needs to be confessed and forgiven; then you will be able to pray together.

A second reason couples are unable to pray together may be that one or both of them have never learned to pray with another person. To many people, prayer is private. While you should pray in private *for* your spouse, you should also pray *with* your spouse. After all, Jesus told his disciples that if even two or three of them were gathered together, he would be present among them. That's a powerful statement and a great testimony to praying together as a couple.

An easy way to get started is with silent prayer. It works like this: You hold hands, close your eyes, then pray silently. When you have finished praying, you say, "Amen," and then wait until your spouse says, "Amen." Praying silently while holding hands is one way of praying together, and it will enhance your marriage.

◆ ◆ ◆

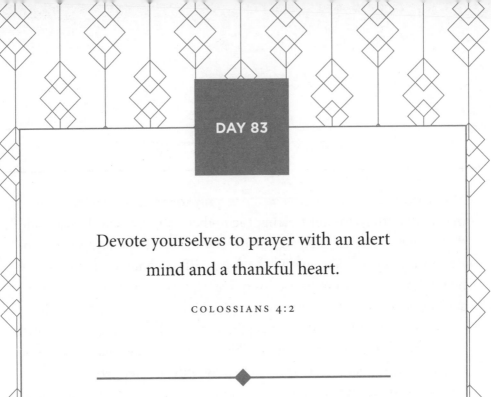

Devote yourselves to prayer with an alert
mind and a thankful heart.

COLOSSIANS 4:2

---

*Father God, I am amazed that I can talk to you at any time,
and you hear me! What an incredible gift. Please help us to
use this gift as a couple. I know that praying together will
help us grow in our love for you and our love for each other.
Give us the courage to get started and the discipline to
continue.*

CONVERSATIONAL PRAYER

THE BIBLE MAKES CLEAR THAT prayer is important. In Colossians 4, the apostle Paul encourages believers to "devote" themselves to prayer; in another epistle, he tells believers to pray continually (see 1 Thessalonians 5:17). We often take prayer for granted, but it's really an amazing concept. We can talk directly to the Creator of the universe! Why wouldn't we want to make that a habit with our spouse?

In the previous devotion, I talked about praying silently together with your spouse. It's the easiest way to get started. Today, I want to encourage you to try *conversational prayer*. In this approach, the two of you take turns talking to God. You may each pray one or more times about the same subject. Then one of you changes the subject, and you repeat the process. It's talking to God like you would talk to a friend.

For example, the husband might pray, "Father God, thank you for protecting me on the way home from work today." The wife might then pray, "Yes, Father, I know that there are many accidents each day, and I sometimes take your protection for granted. I also want to thank you for protecting the children today." The husband prays, "I agree, and I pray especially that you will protect our kids from those who would pull them away from their faith." The wife prays, "Oh, Father, give us wisdom in how to teach our children to know and love you." And so the conversation with God continues. It is an exciting way to pray with your spouse. Not only will it draw you closer to your heavenly Father, but it will draw you and your spouse closer together as you hear and pray about each other's concerns.

We know how dearly God loves us, because he has given us the Holy Spirit to fill our hearts with his love.

ROMANS 5:5

Heavenly Father, thank you for filling my heart with your love. No matter how frustrated I am with my marriage, I want to commit to loving my spouse unconditionally for the next six months and speaking his or her love language. Please give me the determination to do this. I know you can transform my marriage.

EXPRESSING LOVE TO THE UNLOVELY

HOW CAN WE LOVE AN UNLOVELY SPOUSE? Through almost thirty years of counseling, I have met with many individuals who live in unbelievably difficult marriages. Without exception, the root problem of marital difficulties is selfishness, and the root cure is love. Love and selfishness are opposites. By nature, we are all self-centered, but when we become Christians, the Holy Spirit brings the love of God into our hearts, as Romans 5:5 indicates. Galatians 5 lists the character qualities the Holy Spirit will produce in our lives if we allow him, and these include love. We now can become God's agents for expressing his love. Sharing this divine love flowing through us is the most powerful thing we can do for our spouse.

I want to give you the challenge I have given many people through the years. Try a six-month experiment of loving your spouse unconditionally. Discover your spouse's primary love language and speak it at least once a week for six months, no matter how you are treated in return. I have seen hard, harsh, cruel people melt long before the six months are over. When you let God express his love through you, you can become the agent of healing for your spouse and your marriage.

◆ ◆ ◆

Wise words bring many benefits, and hard work brings rewards. Fools think their own way is right, but the wise listen to others.

PROVERBS 12:14-15

Father, thank you for these ideas on how to compromise. Please help me to let go of my need to do things my way. You know that I love my spouse and want to respect his or her ideas. I want to commit to loving compromise as we make decisions.

FINDING COMPROMISE

IN MAKING DECISIONS, husbands and wives often disagree. If we don't learn how to come together, we may spend a lifetime fighting. Agreement requires listening, understanding, and compromise. Compromise expresses a willingness to move. It is the opposite of being rigid. King Solomon said it bluntly in Proverbs 12: "Fools think their own way is right, but the wise listen to others." If we respect our spouse as our partner, we should also respect his or her viewpoint. It's neither wise nor loving to cling to our own viewpoint to the exclusion of our mate.

There are three possible ways to resolve a disagreement. One is what I call "Meet you on your side." In other words, you might say, "Now that I see how important this is to you, I'm willing to do what you want." You agree to do it your spouse's way for his or her benefit.

A second possibility is "Meet you in the middle." This means you might say, "I'd be willing to give a little if you could give a little, and we'll meet in the middle." For example, "I'll go with you to your mother's for the Friday night dinner if you will return with me Saturday morning in time for the big game."

The third possibility is "Meet you later." A couple in this position might say, "We don't seem to be making any progress. Why don't we just agree to disagree and discuss it again next week?" In the meantime, call a truce and treat each other kindly.

◆ ◆ ◆

"Don't sin by letting anger control you." Don't let the sun go down while you are still angry, for anger gives a foothold to the devil.

EPHESIANS 4:26-27

Heavenly Father, you know that I sometimes hold on to a grudge against my spouse. Please help me to stop! Remind me to stop my response, figure out why I'm angry, and then decide whether to bring it up with my spouse or to let it go. I need wisdom, Lord, so I don't let anger take control of me.

LETTING ANGER GO

IT HAPPENS TO ALL OF US. We get bent out of shape by some little comment or action of our spouse. She let the dog out without a leash, and now the neighbor is calling to complain. He left his socks on the floor instead of moving six inches to put them into the laundry hamper. It's the little things that stimulate distorted anger.

How do we handle our emotions? First, we admit them. "I'm feeling angry." Second, we refuse to let the anger control us. "So I'm going to take a walk." Third, we ask ourselves some key questions. *Did my spouse do this on purpose? Was he trying to hurt me? Or is this simply the result of being married to a human? Have I done similar things in the past? Is this big enough to talk with my spouse about, or shall I let it go?*

Either let it go or talk with your spouse about it. Don't hold anger inside. The Bible warns that we should get rid of anger before dark. When we hold on to anger, it has a tendency to start controlling us—and, as Paul writes, that gives a "foothold to the devil." In other words, holding on to anger makes us likely to sin more and more. Our anger becomes increasingly distorted, and that paves the way for all sorts of ugly interactions in a marriage. Anger should be treated as a visitor, never a resident.

◆ ◆ ◆

If the whole body were an eye, how would you hear?
Or if your whole body were an ear, how would you
smell anything? But our bodies have many parts,
and God has put each part just where he wants it.

1 CORINTHIANS 12:17-18

◆

*Father, thank you for the differences between me and my
spouse. Please show me how to look at them positively
rather than negatively. Help us to work effectively together
as a team.*

CELEBRATING DIFFERENCES

DIFFERENCES CAN BE DELIGHTFUL. An old adage says, "Some people read history; others make it." Usually, these two types of people are married to each other. Now I ask you, isn't that the way God designed it?

Our differences are meant to be complementary. How tragic it would be if your spouse were just like you. God tends to place an aggressive person with a more passive person, a neatnik with a slob, an organized person with a spontaneous person. Why? Because we need each other. It's sad when we allow our differences to become divisive. Why do we do this? Because we are egocentric. *Life revolves around me*, we think. *My way is the best way. Be like me, and we'll be happy!*

But is that really what we want? I don't think so. In 1 Corinthians 12, the apostle Paul compares the church to a body. It has many parts, and every part is needed. Paul takes this illustration almost to absurdity, asking his readers to imagine how the body would function if it were just one great big ear. It wouldn't! How limited life would be.

The same holds true in marriage. We are different, and we need each other. Your aggressiveness pushes me to attempt things I would never try on my own. My passiveness keeps you from jumping off the cliff. The Bible is right: Two are better than one.

◆ ◆ ◆

Be thankful in all circumstances, for this is God's
will for you who belong to Christ Jesus.

1 THESSALONIANS 5:18

*Father God, you have made today, and I will choose to
rejoice in it regardless of my circumstances. I know you
have good plans for me, and I am thankful that I can choose
to use this day for good. Please help me to turn away from
the negativity that only makes me miserable. I want to learn
to see you in my circumstances.*

LIVING IN THE PRESENT

IF YOU'RE IN A CHALLENGING MARRIAGE, you may be tempted to flee; but you know there must be a better way. There is, and it comes from making the most of what you have, one day at a time. Don't spoil your future by allowing bitterness to consume your spirit. Don't destroy yourself with self-pity. Don't drive your friends away by constantly refusing their comfort.

You can make your life miserable by focusing on your problems. Or you can say with the psalmist, "This is the day the LORD has made. We will rejoice and be glad in it" (Psalm 118:24). You may not be able to rejoice over the past or over your present situation, but you can rejoice that God has given you the ability to use this day for good. You can also follow the apostle Paul's challenge from 1 Thessalonians 5:18 to "be thankful in all circumstances." That doesn't mean you must be thankful *for* all circumstances, but that in every situation, you can choose to see something for which to thank God. He is present in your circumstances, and the more you look for him, the more you will find him.

Don't try to live all of your future today. Jesus emphasized the importance of living one day at a time (see Matthew 6:34). Some good questions to ask yourself are *What can I do today that may improve my situation? What do I need to pray about today? With whom do I need to talk today? What action do I need to take today?* God has entrusted to you only the present, and wise use of today is all that he expects.

◆ ◆ ◆

Come, let us worship and bow down. Let us kneel before the LORD our maker, for he is our God. We are the people he watches over, the flock under his care. If only you would listen to his voice today!

PSALM 95:6-7

Lord Jesus, I know that each day presents a choice. I can concentrate on my past struggles and remain in the same place, or I can choose to make a positive change. Please give me the courage and determination to make the right choices today. May my small steps forward bring our marriage to a stronger, more loving place.

MAKING THE MOST OF TODAY

IN A DIFFICULT MARRIAGE, we are tempted to wallow in our pain. Each day becomes a rerun of the past. But in God's economy, each day is an opportunity for change. Do a search for *today* in the Bible, and you'll find a long list of occasions when people were presented with a choice. That very day they could choose between following God or turning away, between listening to his voice or ignoring it. (See Psalm 95 and Deuteronomy 11:26-27 for just a few examples.) What they did "today" would set the tone for the days to follow. It's the same for you. All of your life cannot be straightened out today; but if you make the most of it, you can work on cleaning up one corner of your life. Choose a corner that you think is most important right now.

As you clean up the corners of your life day by day, all of life begins to look brighter. You cannot change your spouse? Then change your attitude about your spouse's behavior. Change your own behavior by confessing past failures. Ask God to help you do one kind deed for your spouse today. You cannot *change* your spouse, but you can *influence* your spouse. One act of kindness each day is likely to change the climate in your relationship, and eventually it may influence your spouse to reciprocate.

Never give up. There is always something good that can be done today. Making the most of today is the most powerful thing you can do for a better tomorrow.

◆ ◆ ◆

Make me truly happy by agreeing wholeheartedly with each other, loving one another, and working together with one mind and purpose.

PHILIPPIANS 2:2

◆

Lord God, I am grateful for my spouse and for the chance to work as a team to keep our household and family running smoothly. I want to help my spouse succeed, Lord. Please guide us as we come up with a plan for handling responsibilities. Help me to communicate in love.

WORKING AS A TEAM

MANY COUPLES ENTER MARRIAGE with the assumption that their household will be run the way their parents did it. The problem is, there are two moms and dads, and they probably didn't do things the same way. Your parents and your spouse's parents didn't have the same game plan; so as husband and wife, you naturally have very different expectations. What's the answer? You must construct your own game plan along with your spouse.

Make a list of all the household responsibilities that come to your mind. Washing dishes, cooking meals, buying groceries, vacuuming the carpet, washing the car, mowing the grass, paying the bills—everything. Ask your spouse to do the same. Then put your two lists together and come up with a "master list" of responsibilities. Next, each of you should take the list and put your initials by the things you think should be your responsibilities. Finally, get together and see where you agree. The differences will need to be negotiated, with someone being willing to take responsibility.

Try it for six months and then evaluate how things are going. Do you feel the responsibilities are divided fairly? Is one person struggling with a certain task that perhaps the other could do more easily? What changes need to be made?

As you talk through these issues, remember that you're on the same team. As Ecclesiastes 4 says, two people working together can help each other succeed. Isn't that what you want for your marriage? Use your strengths to help each other.

◆ ◆ ◆

When I refused to confess my sin, my body wasted
away, and I groaned all day long. . . . Finally, I
confessed all my sins to you and stopped trying to
hide my guilt. I said to myself, "I will confess my
rebellion to the LORD." And you forgave me!
All my guilt is gone.

PSALM 32:3, 5

*God, sometimes it's so hard to humble myself to say a simple,
"I'm sorry." Help me not to take my spouse's forgiveness for
granted, but to be willing to admit when I am wrong.*

THE POWER OF APOLOGY

LOVE STORY, THE CLASSIC SEVENTIES MOVIE, advised us that "love means never having to say you're sorry." I don't think they got it right, for one simple reason: We are all human, and humans are not perfect. All of us end up hurting the people we love most. Having a good marriage does not demand perfection, but it does require us to apologize when we fail.

When I say, "I'm sorry," I'm expressing regret that my words or behavior have brought you pain. It's a basic guideline for getting along with others. It also reflects the spiritual truth that to receive forgiveness, we first need to admit what we've done. Ignoring our sin doesn't make it go away, as King David experienced before he wrote the words of Psalm 32. In fact, ignoring it often makes us feel far worse. But when we express regret for our wrongdoing and the hurt it caused, we pave the way for forgiveness and reconciliation. That's true in our relationship with God as well as in our marriage.

When was the last time you said, "I'm sorry," to your husband or wife? If it's been a while, then you probably owe him or her an apology. Love means always being willing to say, "I'm sorry."

◆ ◆ ◆

The ear tests the words it hears just as the mouth
distinguishes between foods.

JOB 12:11

◆

*Lord, often I need to go the extra mile to make amends.
Help me to show my spouse that I am sincere, and that I
desire to do what is right. Help me to be willing to seek the
reconciliation that our relationship needs.*

BEYOND "I'M SORRY"

PERHAPS YOU HAVE SAID, "I'm sorry," but your spouse is finding it hard to forgive you. You may feel frustrated and say to yourself, *I apologized. What else can I do?* If you're serious, I'll tell you. Ask your spouse this question: "What can I do to make this up to you?" You might also say, "I know I hurt you, and I feel badly about it, but I want to make it right. I want to do something to show you that I love you."

This is far more powerful than simply saying, "I'm sorry." Why? Because sometimes words don't mean much unless they're backed up with action. In the Old Testament book that bears his name, Job is overrun with words from his friends, who try to make sense of his terrible suffering. But much of what they say is wrong, and in today's passage, Job says that he tested their words to determine what was true. We all do the same thing—test words to see if they are genuine and if they will likely be followed up with action.

To establish trust, you need to show that your words are genuine. When you ask your spouse how you can make the situation right, you are trying to make restitution. You are demonstrating that you really care about your relationship. After all, what your spouse wants to know is whether your apology is sincere. Make sure your answer is clear.

◆ ◆ ◆

Pay attention to how you hear. To those who listen to my teaching, more understanding will be given. But for those who are not listening, even what they think they understand will be taken away from them.

LUKE 8:18

◆

Father, I need to be a better listener—to you as well as to my spouse. Help me to stop my mind and my mouth from moving when it's my loved one's turn to talk. Please give me greater understanding so that we can build greater intimacy.

BUILDING INTIMACY THROUGH LISTENING

BUILDING INTIMACY IS A PROCESS, not an event. We don't obtain intimacy and keep it on the shelf as a treasure for the rest of our lives. Intimacy is fluid, not static. And the way we maintain intimacy is communication.

Communication involves two simple elements: *self-revelation* and *listening*. One person tells the other his or her thoughts, feelings, and experiences (self-revelation) while the other *listens* with a view to understanding what the spouse is thinking and feeling. The process is then reversed, and the speaker becomes the listener. The simple act of talking and listening maintains intimacy.

If this is all it takes, what's the big problem? It's called selfishness. Too often, we stop listening and start preaching. When both partners are preaching, neither preacher has an audience. When we get tired of talking at each other, we withdraw in silent resentment. We will never be able to return to intimacy until we apologize and forgive each other for being selfish.

Jesus talked about listening, as we can see in Luke 8:18. When we listen intently, he said, we gain understanding. But when we aren't paying attention, we lose even the understanding we once had. That's how important genuine listening is in building intimacy.

◆ ◆ ◆

[Jesus said,] "I will show you what it's like when someone comes to me, listens to my teaching, and then follows it. It is like a person building a house who digs deep and lays the foundation on solid rock. When the floodwaters rise and break against that house, it stands firm because it is well built."

LUKE 6:47-48

Father, I want our marriage to have a strong foundation of oneness. Help us to build it up as we seek to develop intimacy in all areas of our relationship. May our marriage be able to withstand the storms that will come our way in this life. Please guide us.

BUILDING A FIRM FOUNDATION

A STRONG FOUNDATION IS THE KEY to a strong marriage. Jesus told the story of a wise person who built a house on a foundation of solid rock. When storms and floods came, the house was not shaken. Contrast that to the foolish person, who built a house with no foundation. It collapsed at the first storm. The foundation in our relationship with God is faith, trust, and obedience. In our marriage, the foundation is oneness.

In God's plan, marriage involves two people, husband and wife, becoming one unit. They choose to share life more deeply with each other than with anyone else. This intimacy involves all aspects of life. Ideally, before we get married, we should explore the foundation for oneness. Intellectually, are we on the same wavelength? Can we talk and understand each other? Emotionally, are we able to share our feelings without fear of rejection? Socially, do we enjoy similar activities? Spiritually, are we marching to the beat of the same drummer?

After marriage, we build on this foundation. If the foundation is shaky, then it will be more difficult to build intimacy. But build we must, for that is the heart of what marriage is all about. If we choose to disengage and live separate lives, we are violating God's design for marriage. Creating intimacy may be difficult, but we have all of God's help when we commit ourselves to following his plan.

◆ ◆ ◆

Three things will last forever—faith, hope, and
love—and the greatest of these is love.

1 CORINTHIANS 13:13

*Lord Jesus, thank you for your love that never fails. And
thank you for the love I can share with my spouse. Please
help me to love effectively, so that he or she will feel secure
in our relationship.*

OUR PRIMARY NEED

LOVE AND MARRIAGE—they go together like a horse and carriage. Right? Well, they should, and in a healthy marriage, they do. Most people agree that our deepest emotional need is to feel loved. The apostle Paul even identifies love as the greatest thing, and King David wrote that God's "unfailing love is better than life itself" (Psalm 63:3). There's no question that God's steady love for us can be our emotional rock. But we also need to experience human love. And if we are married, the person whose love we long for the most is our spouse. In fact, if we feel loved, everything else is workable. If we don't feel loved, our conflicts become battlefields.

Now, don't misunderstand me. I'm not suggesting that love is our only need. Psychologists have observed that we also have basic emotional needs for security, self-worth, and significance. However, love interfaces with all of these.

If I feel loved, then I can relax, knowing that my spouse will do me no ill. I feel secure in his or her presence. I can face the uncertainties in my vocation. I may have enemies in other areas of my life, but with my spouse I feel secure. In the next two days, I'll talk about how to effectively meet your spouse's need for emotional love.

◆ ◆ ◆

See how very much our Father loves us, for he calls
us his children, and that is what we are!

1 JOHN 3:1

*Heavenly Father, thank you for allowing us to call you
Father! You have adopted us as your children, and you care
for us as tenderly as a shepherd cares for sheep. Thank you
for valuing us. Please help me as I strive to communicate
that value to my spouse through my expressions of love.*

UNDERSTANDING OUR VALUE

OFTEN, MARITAL LOVE MAKES THE difference between low self-esteem and healthy self-esteem. Love makes a difference in the way I perceive myself.

In reality, of course, all of us are of great value simply because we are made in the image of God. The apostle John makes clear that God calls us his children because he loves us so much. The Bible also uses the image of sheep. Psalm 100:3 says, "He made us, and we are his. We are his people, the sheep of his pasture." In short, we are loved and valued, we belong, and we are cared for. That's a wonderful message for any believer's self-worth.

But not all of us *feel* valuable. In marriage, we can be God's instrument for building our mate's self-esteem. The best way to do that is to love our spouse and communicate God's truth to him or her. Speaking our spouse's love language and keeping his or her love tank full also communicates worth. After all, if my spouse loves me, I must be worth something.

Do you know your spouse's primary love language—what really makes him or her feel loved? Then ask God to give you the ability to speak that language well, whether it's physical touch, words of affirmation, quality time, gifts, or acts of service. Watch your spouse blossom into the person God intends him or her to be. Love makes a difference.

◆ ◆ ◆

Above all, you must live as citizens of heaven, conducting yourselves in a manner worthy of the Good News about Christ. Then . . . I will know that you are standing together with one spirit and one purpose, fighting together for the faith, which is the Good News.

PHILIPPIANS 1:27

Father, I am thankful for the significance you give me. I want to fulfill your purposes for me and share your love with others. Please help me to start by loving my spouse well and selflessly. Through that, may he or she feel significant too.

FINDING OUR SIGNIFICANCE

The need for significance drives much of our behavior. We want our lives to count for something. In reality, we are significant because God made us. Life does have meaning. There is a higher purpose—to share God's love with others by spreading the Good News. The apostle Paul encouraged believers to be united in this purpose, and that still holds true today. When we communicate God's love, we are doing something highly significant.

However, I may not feel significant until someone expresses love to me. When my spouse lovingly invests time, energy, and effort in me, I feel valuable. But surprisingly, when I choose to love my spouse and give my life for his or her well-being, I feel even more valuable. Why? Because it is more blessed to give than to receive.

Christ is our example. He gave up his life for the church (see Ephesians 5:25); consequently, God "highly exalted Him" (Philippians 2:9, NKJV). One of your greatest contributions to the cause of Christ is to love your spouse.

◆ ◆ ◆

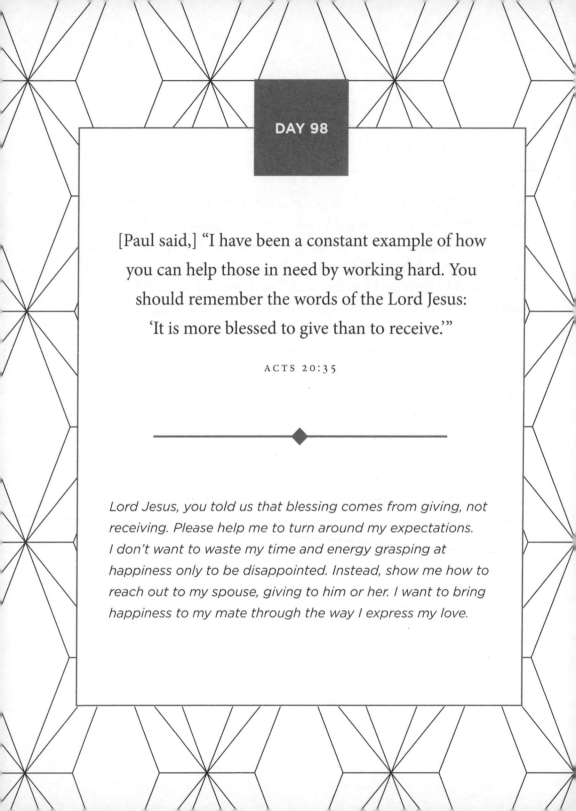

DAY 98

[Paul said,] "I have been a constant example of how you can help those in need by working hard. You should remember the words of the Lord Jesus: 'It is more blessed to give than to receive.'"

ACTS 20:35

Lord Jesus, you told us that blessing comes from giving, not receiving. Please help me to turn around my expectations. I don't want to waste my time and energy grasping at happiness only to be disappointed. Instead, show me how to reach out to my spouse, giving to him or her. I want to bring happiness to my mate through the way I express my love.

LOVE DOES NOT SEEK ITS OWN

HAPPINESS IS A UNIQUE COMMODITY. It is never found by the person shopping for it. Lonely men and women in every age have admitted the futility of their search for happiness, most notably King Solomon in the book of Ecclesiastes. This wealthy, powerful king, with servants to cater to his every whim, found most things in life to be tedious, meaningless, and devoid of joy.

Most of us get married assuming that we are going to be happy. After the wedding, we find that our mate does not always seek to make us happy. Perhaps our spouse even demands more and more of our time, energy, and resources for his or her own happiness. We feel cheated and used, so we fight for our rights. We demand that our spouse do certain things for us, or we give up and seek happiness elsewhere.

Part of the apostle Paul's definition of love in 1 Corinthians 13 is that it is "not self-seeking" (verse 5, NIV). Genuine happiness is the by-product of making someone else happy. I wonder what would have happened if King Solomon had found someone to serve? Doesn't Acts 20:35 say, "It is more blessed to give than to receive"?

Do you want to be happy? Discover someone else's needs and seek to meet them. Why not begin with your spouse? "How may I help you?" is a good question with which to begin.

❖ ❖ ❖

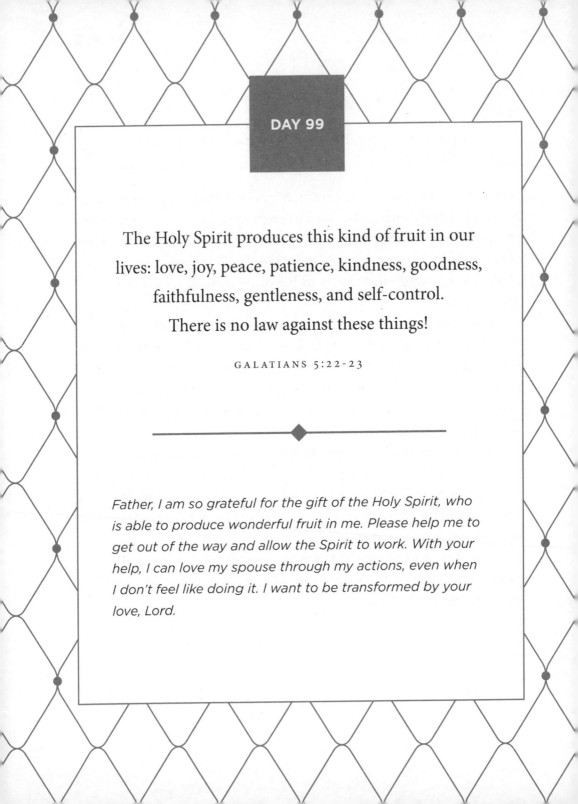

DAY 99

The Holy Spirit produces this kind of fruit in our lives: love, joy, peace, patience, kindness, goodness, faithfulness, gentleness, and self-control. There is no law against these things!

GALATIANS 5:22-23

Father, I am so grateful for the gift of the Holy Spirit, who is able to produce wonderful fruit in me. Please help me to get out of the way and allow the Spirit to work. With your help, I can love my spouse through my actions, even when I don't feel like doing it. I want to be transformed by your love, Lord.

TRANSFORMING POWER OF LOVE

THE STORY IS TOLD OF A WOMAN who went to a marriage counselor for advice. "I want to divorce my husband," she said, "and I want to hurt him as much as I can."

"In that case," the counselor advised, "start showering him with compliments. When you have become indispensable to him—when he thinks you love him devotedly—then start the divorce action. That's the way to hurt him most."

Some months later, the wife returned to report that she had followed the counselor's advice.

"Good," said the counselor. "Now's the time to file for divorce."

"Divorce?" said the woman. "Never! I've fallen in love with the guy."

Loving words and actions change not only the spouse; they change the one speaking and acting lovingly. Didn't Jesus say, "Love your enemies" (Matthew 5:44)? Perhaps your spouse qualifies, at least at certain moments! It may seem impossible, but Galatians 5 reassures us that it's not all up to us. The Holy Spirit, who dwells within believers, produces godly attributes in us: love, joy, peace, patience, kindness, goodness, faithfulness, gentleness, and self-control. What a list! All we need to do is allow him to work within us.

Loving your spouse in the power of the Holy Spirit will never make things worse. Who knows? Things may get better. Go against your emotions and give love a chance.

◆ ◆ ◆

Follow my example, as I follow the example of Christ.

1 CORINTHIANS 11:1 (NIV)

◆

Lord Jesus, I know that the only way I can leave a strong legacy is by following your example. Please help me to become more and more like you in the way I treat my spouse and the way I approach our marriage. I want to leave a positive example for those around us. Thank you, Lord.

WHAT IS YOUR LEGACY?

AMONG THE THINGS YOU WILL leave behind when you die is a marital legacy. Your example will without a doubt influence the lives of your children and others who observe it. Few things are more important than building the kind of marriage that you would be happy to have your children emulate.

When I ask older parents, "What do you wish for your adult children?" their response is often, "I want them to be happily married and to rear their children to be loving, caring citizens." That's a worthy goal. What are you doing to foster that goal? I want to suggest that the model of your own marriage is the greatest factor in helping your children have happy marriages.

The question is, will you leave a positive or a negative legacy? Many young adults struggle greatly because of the influence of the negative example set by their parents' marriage. Others are blessed greatly by a positive model.

It is not too late. As long as you are alive, you have time to work on the marital legacy you will leave behind. The best thing we can do is what Paul did: follow the example of Christ. The more closely we follow Jesus and treat each other the way he calls us to, the more Christlike our legacy will be.

◆ ◆ ◆

TOPICAL INDEX

SCRIPTURE INDEX

ABOUT THE AUTHOR

Dr. Gary Chapman is the author of the perennial bestseller *The Five Love Languages* (over six million copies sold) and numerous other marriage and family books. He also coauthored a fiction series based on *The Four Seasons of Marriage* with bestselling author Catherine Palmer. Dr. Chapman is the director of Marriage and Family Life Consultants, Inc.; an internationally known speaker; and the host of *A Love Language Minute*, a syndicated radio program heard on more than two hundred stations across North America. He and his wife, Karolyn, live in North Carolina.

ALSO AVAILABLE
— FROM —
GARY CHAPMAN

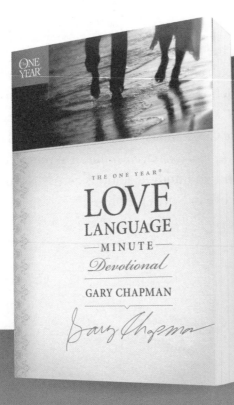

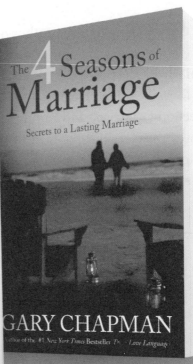